Puffin Books

All the Year Round

CW00864872

Can you make yourself in[visible?] [...] thing to do with old socks [...] [way of] making exploding snacks? How can you keep witches away?

If you don't know the answers to any of these questions then you've simply got to read this book. You'll learn about midsummer rituals, dragon puppets, gingerbread men and magic rites with everyday objects.

Television presenter and singer, Toni Arthur, has compiled an incredible variety of traditional customs and stories, songs and games to keep you occupied and interested during even the greyest times of the year. There are bits of folk lore from all over Britain which make you realize what a rich and peculiar past this country has. But whilst informing and entertaining you with traditional stories and pastimes, Toni is ever practical. She tells you how to make anything from a sock puppet to cinnamon toast, and she also reveals the secret of invisibility and a foolproof method of keeping witches away.

Children of all ages will love this book. The activities range from the very simple, requiring only pencil and paper, to the more complicated which may require some help from adults.

Explore each month of the year with Toni Arthur and you need never be bored again!

Toni Arthur
All the Year Round

Illustrated by Lyn Jones

Puffin Books

Puffin Books, Penguin Books Ltd, Harmondsworth, Middlesex, England
Penguin Books, 625 Madison Avenue, New York, New York 10022, U.S.A.
Penguin Books Australia Ltd, Ringwood, Victoria, Australia
Penguin Books Canada Ltd, 2801 John Street, Markham, Ontario, Canada L3R 1B4
Penguin Books (N.Z.) Ltd, 182–190 Wairau Road, Auckland 10, New Zealand

Published in Puffin Books 1981
Reprinted 1982

Made and printed in Great Britain by
Richard Clay (The Chaucer Press) Ltd, Bungay, Suffolk
Set in Monotype Baskerville

For Dave

Foreword

Toni Arthur is one of my favourite people on television. She's friendly and sparky and full of bright ideas. You'll probably know her best from *Play School* and *Play Away* which she presented for nine years. Now she's come up with the great notion of a book that's crammed with things to do every month of the year. It's going to be a vital addition to my family's book collection because it's got tips and information to fill those times of year – and there are lots of them – when not much seems to be happening.

There are many books covering the special times like Christmas, but this one gives just as much space to the quieter months. And in compiling her book, Toni has uncovered dozens of stories that are new to me about the history and folk lore of Britain.

Toni's amazing range of talents and interests more than equip her to write a book like this. She trained as a classical musician, actress, nurse and photographer and has a flourishing singing partnership with her husband, Dave.

With a tremendous enthusiasm for our heritage, Toni is determined to revive customs and traditions that bring people together. Her passion for folk lore extends to a library of over 6,000 books and a vast collection of records and tapes.

This book is Toni's way of publicizing the richness of Britain's past and encouraging us to participate in it. As you'll discover, the book is filled with fascinating information. In fact, Toni has turned the year into an adventurous journey, with lots of stops along the way for games, songs, stories and things to make. At the same time, she's doing a great service by digging up some of the almost forgotten legends and pastimes that stem from this country's delightful and often quirky folk history. Thanks to this book, they are now being passed on to a new generation which otherwise might not have heard about them. Let's hope you keep them alive.

My tip is to read this book all the way through and then put it carefully on one side and bring it out every month. That way you'll have a delightful guide from January through to December, and you'll have no excuse for saying you have nothing to do on a quiet day during a dull month.

JOHN CRAVEN

Introduction

This book is written for all those young people who say, as I always used to, 'I'm bored. What can I do?' There are things to make, things to do, stories to read, songs to sing and some awful jokes that I hope will make you laugh. (Actually, I made up some of the jokes myself. I wonder if you can guess which ones they are – my children say it's obvious!)

When you're making any of the things from this book you don't have to use exactly the same equipment as I used. Sometimes it might suit you more to use Blu-Tack instead of glue, and remnants of wallpaper instead of wrapping paper. Experiment for yourself – it's more exciting that way.

REMEMBER – put old cloth or newspapers over the work surface and floors before you start making things. Being told off for making a mess could cut short your career as an artist or sculptor!

Acknowledgements

It takes a long time to write a book, and although the main ideas come from one person (in this case, me) it can't be finished without the help of many others – so I would like to thank those people who have helped me.

First of all, my husband, Dave, for telling me that I *could* write it and for buying all the many books that I needed for my research. Secondly, our two sons, Jonathan and Timothy, who listened patiently and offered advice while I read them each chapter and showed them everything I'd made.

When the book was finished, it was typed and retyped by Heather Bader and Marian Gray, and Jenny McKay drew pictures based on my very rough sketches.

Finally, the Puffin staff put their clever minds to work, corrected the words, and found Lyn Jones who did all the super illustrations.

P.S. One more thank you – to my mum and dad – just for being them.

TONI ARTHUR 1981

The January Man

Wrap up warm, January man,
For the cold north wind does blow,
The sky is dark, the trees are bare,
And the grass is covered with snow.

Icicles glisten from the trees
And the first snowdrops appear;
February man builds a snowman tall
To give himself some cheer.

Strong winds blow the man of March
As he climbs up the hill,
But he's happy to watch the grasses dance
With the yellow daffodil.

Birds come in from across the sea,
And the gardens begin to flower,
But the April man still watches out
For a sudden rainy shower.

Children play beneath a tree
That's covered with flowering cherry;
The sun peeps out from behind a cloud
To make the May man merry.

In June the man walks with his dog
Among tall corn and flowers,
And sits a while, and chats a while
To pass away the hours.

The July man rests under the leaves,
For the sun is high in the sky,
The air is sweet with summer smells,
And a busy bee flies by.

The August man with everyman
Rushes to cool by the sea;
His feet are bare, the sand is warm,
There's no happier man than he.

Holiday's over, September man,
There's work to be done on the land,
Food to get ready for winter time,
There's no time to sit or stand.

Gather the apples, October man,
And the autumn leaves need clearing,
The days are short, the nights are long,
And Hallowe'en is nearing.

Fog wraps round November man,
It's cold and damp and dark;
A ship's horn blows far out at sea
And a lonely dog does bark.

Time to go home, December man,
Home to your family and friends,
To sing and be merry at party time
As the old year ends.

1980   TONI ARTHUR

January

Wrap up warm, January man,
For the cold north wind does blow,
The sky is dark, the trees are bare,
And the grass is covered with snow.

The beginning of a new year, and the time to make New Year resolutions such as:

1 This year I will not bite my fingernails.
2 This year I really *will* help in the garden.
3 This year I will try hard at school.
4 This year I will clean my teeth every day.

Almost everyone makes New Year promises to themselves. In fact they try to treat the New Year as you would treat a new exercise book – it's just a way of starting things afresh.

In the old days, the New Year started with a custom called 'first footing', which was supposed to bring good luck to people for the coming year. As soon as midnight had passed and January 1st had started, people used to wait behind their doors for a dark-haired person to arrive. The visitor carried a piece of coal, some bread, some money and some greenery. These were all for good luck – the coal to make sure that the house would always be warm, the bread to make sure that everyone in the house would have enough food to eat, money so that they would have enough money, and the greenery to make sure that they had a long life.

You could do this today. You could go round to the houses that you know and call in to bring good luck; if you haven't got dark hair, you could put a dark woolly cap on.

Perhaps you would rather go and visit people's houses with a group of your friends. Groups of children used to sing songs as they went round, rather like the carol singers at Christmas time, but at New Year they were called 'wassailers'. That's because they used to carry with them a 'wassail bowl' full of a spicy drink made from beer, oranges, lemons, herbs and spices, which they gave to their neighbours in exchange for some pennies or a piece of cake.

If you can't take a bowl full of 'spiced ale', as it was called, you could take some nuts or some shiny pennies to give as New Year gifts and you could say a verse from an old wassail song as you knock at the door.

> *We are not daily beggars*
> *That beg from door to door*
> *But we are neighbours' children*
> *That you have seen before.*
> *Love and joy come to you,*
> *And to you your wassail too,*
> *And God send you a Happy New Year.*

You'll be surprised how happy this will make your neighbours, and they may even forget that your football went through their window last year!

Wassail Bowl

Wassailers went on visiting and singing until Twelfth Night. That's the last day of the Christmas celebrations and it's on January 6th. One of the last things that people used to do, to make sure that the new year would be all right, was to wassail the apple trees. They would dance round an apple tree shouting things like:

> *Stand fast root.*
> *Bear well top.*
> *Pray God send us a howling good crop!*
> *Every twig apples big,*
> *Every bough apples enow (enough).*
> *Hats full, caps full,*
> *Full quarter sacks full.*
> *Holla boys, holla, huzzah.*

After shouting this rhyme, they would then make as many loud noises as they could by banging tin trays, knocking saucepan lids together and firing guns to frighten away evil spirits that they thought might harm the apple trees. Cider (which is a drink made from apples) was then poured over the roots of the tree and a piece of toast was dipped in the cider and placed on a branch of the tree. I wonder if this type of 'magic' really worked? Perhaps you could try it for yourself. If you have an apple tree growing near, you might be able to get permission to try it out. It could be fun to go shouting the old rhyme and banging a tin tray, and then you could climb the tree to place a slice of toast soaked in cider or apple juice on one of the branches. If nothing else happens I should think the birds would like to eat the toast. You never know, perhaps the tree will have so much fruit because of what you've done that you will be given a lot of apples later on in the year.

After being out in the cold weather of January it would be great to come home to a wassail cup of your own to warm you up again. Here's a recipe for one; it will make enough for you and your friends.

Wassail Cup

You need :   Large saucepan
Large bowl
Cups and a jug

2 oranges
2 lemons
2 apples
4 fl oz (56 cc) undiluted orange squash
4 fl oz (56 cc) undiluted lemon squash
1 teaspoonful cinnamon
Pinch ginger powder
4 cloves
2 teaspoonsful honey
2 pints (1 litre) water

What to do : 1 Peel and chop the fruit into small pieces and remove the pips.

2 Put all the chopped fruit, squashes, spices and honey into the saucepan and add the water.

3 Put the saucepan on the cooker and bring the mixture to the boil. (You may need to get someone to help you with this.)

4 Simmer for about 5 minutes.

5 Turn off the gas or electricity and leave the drink to cool down a little.

6 Pour into a large bowl.

7 Dip a jug into the bowl and pour the drink into cups.

Now you have a warm spicy drink with lumps of fruit in it to chew, very like the drink that the wassailers used to have many years ago.

As January 6th comes to an end, it's time to take down the Christmas decorations, the Christmas tree and the Christmas cards, as it's supposed to be bad luck to leave the decorations up after Twelfth Night; if you take them down too soon it's bad luck too, for that means you won't have much money in the year to come. So, if you want to make sure your pocket money's safe, take the decorations down exactly on Twelfth Night!

Now the fun of Christmas is over, one of the first things that has to be done is . . . TIDY YOUR ROOM ! ! !

New toys and games have to find a home and old broken ones have to be thrown away. But before you start throwing away, why don't you find a secret hiding place for 'Things That Might Be Useful'. This could be an empty drawer, a

box under the bed, the bottom of the wardrobe – or just clear all the rubbish off a shelf or the window-sill and use that. WARNING: If it looks untidy, it may be mistaken for rubbish and thrown away! So label it . . . carefully!

Hiding place at the ready, let's start collecting useful things.

1 Cut out and save all the best pictures from your Christmas cards and then throw the rest away.
2 Save all the best, uncreased bits of wrapping paper and fold them away neatly.
3 Roll up any good pieces of string or ribbon and stop the ends from running away by putting elastic bands round them.
4 Before you throw away old broken toys, look out for any pieces of wood or board that have managed to stay in one piece and save them. But remember, BROKEN BITS OF WOOD AND METAL ARE DANGEROUS, SO THROW THEM AWAY . . . NOW!

Right, now you've started a treasure chest, let's find out what we can make from the things that are around us in January.

Oranges

If you haven't used up all the oranges left over from Christmas by making a wassail drink, ask for two more and you can make them into pomanders.

Pomanders were first used in France as a protection against the plague. They are balls of sweet-smelling herbs and spices, and at one time it was thought that a good, nice smell would chase away a bad and harmful smell. In other words, people used to think that a pomander would act as a disinfectant and kill off germs.

In Shakespeare's time the pedlars or 'travelling salesmen' would go round the markets selling pomanders made from all sorts of exotic perfumes, and I should think the people really needed them in those days because full chamber pots would be thrown into the streets and there were no fridges to keep food fresh. The air of a market must have smelled a bit strong!

Queen Elizabeth I used to have a pomander hanging from a belt round her waist, or from a chain around her neck, which she could just lift close to her nose if some of her subjects seemed a little too smelly.

Other people used to have pomanders hanging from the ceilings of their rooms or in their wardrobes to make all the air around them smell sweet.

Today we don't need to chase away so many bad smells, but it's still a good idea to have some pleasant smells around. *Let's make some pomanders.*

You need: An orange
Sellotape
A matchstick or knitting needle
Mixed spice
40 cloves
Some ribbon or string (from your
    secret hiding place)

What to do :

1 Mark out the orange with the sellotape as shown.

2 Make a pattern of holes in the spaces between the tape with the end of a matchstick or knitting needle. The holes must not be too wide.

3 Remove the tape. Then as the juice of the orange begins to ooze out of the holes, roll it on a plate on which you have sprinkled two teaspoonsful of mixed spice or cinnamon and ginger, until all the holes become clogged up with the spices.

4 Push a clove into each of the holes and then wrap the orange in tissue or kitchen paper (toilet roll will do) and put it away somewhere safe and dry. A corner of your treasure chest would be ideal. Leave it there for five weeks. During this time, the orange will become hard and dry, and it will look quite a bit smaller. When that happens, the finishing touches must be added.

5 Tie string or ribbon around the orange, leaving enough string over so that the orange can be hung up. Ribbon, of course, is prettier but string works just as well. The finished pomander looks like this and smells lovely.

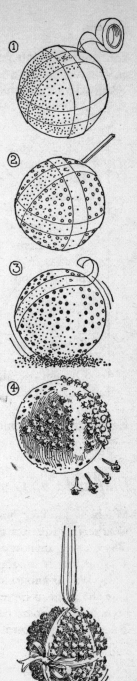

You can hang your pomander in your wardrobe to make it smell good. Make another pomander and hide it in your secret place. You'll find out why later!

Knock, knock.
Who's there?
Banana.
Banana who?

Knock, knock.
Who's there?
Banana.
Banana who?

Knock, knock.
Who's there?
Orange.
Orange who?
Orange you glad I didn't say banana again?

Ugh! Let's make something else.

Ball and Cup Game

Much of January has to be spent indoors because of the weather, so this is a game for you to make which you can play on your own or as a competition with your friends. It's a game that is very old and probably started in Greece or Italy. We do know that King Henry III of France used to play the game as he walked through the streets in 1585. The French name for it was *bilboquet* (pronounced *bilbowkay*) and it was a great favourite with children in Victorian times.

You need: A cardboard tube from the inside of a kitchen
foil holder
Glue or sellotape
String
Cotton wool

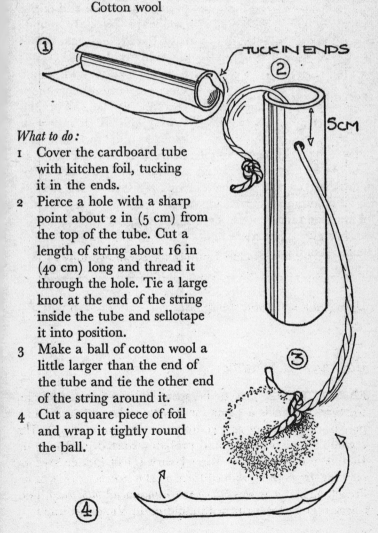

What to do:

1 Cover the cardboard tube
with kitchen foil, tucking
it in the ends.

2 Pierce a hole with a sharp
point about 2 in (5 cm) from
the top of the tube. Cut a
length of string about 16 in
(40 cm) long and thread it
through the hole. Tie a large
knot at the end of the string
inside the tube and sellotape
it into position.

3 Make a ball of cotton wool a
little larger than the end of
the tube and tie the other end
of the string around it.

4 Cut a square piece of foil
and wrap it tightly round
the ball.

Now you are ready to play with your ball and cup game.

The idea of the game is to toss the ball in the air and try to catch it on the end of the cardboard tube. It sounds easy, but in fact it takes quite a while to do. You could have competitions with your friends to see how many times you can get the ball in the 'cup'. This is definitely a game to practise before you show it to your friends. You'll be surprised how many adults also like to play this game, so perhaps you had better make more than one and put them in your treasure chest for later.

The old games were made of wood and ivory, were very elaborately carved and looked like this:

Knock, knock.
Who's there?
Bill.
Bill who?
Bil Bow Kay.

Get it?!

February

Icicles glisten from the trees
And the first snowdrops appear;
February man builds a snowman tall
To give himself some cheer.

Dull old February – the Easter holidays seem to be years away. People are sniffing and coughing and the weather is awful! How can poor February be made exciting?

February used to be a time when lots of things went on, but most of them have been forgotten now – so let's start some of them up again.

February 2nd is Candlemas Day and there used to be many different customs on this date. One of the most interesting customs took place in Scotland. In olden times, Candlemas was the day when children brought candles to school so that the classrooms could have light on dull days. As time went on, gas lighting and then electric lighting took over from candle light. The children took money to the teacher who was supposed to spend it on sweets and cakes for the children to eat. The boy and girl taking in the most money were declared Candlemas King and Queen and they 'ruled' for six weeks. They had the power to make one whole afternoon a week a playtime and they could also let anyone they wished off a punishment.

I think it's a smashing idea! So, how do you go about starting it?

First of all you'll have to ask your teacher if it's all right with him or her. You'll have to say that for the sake of 'history' you don't want old customs to die out and, having convinced the teacher, off you go!

Make February 1st 'Odd job for Candlemas Day' and, charging about 5p a job, try to get a competition going in your class to see who can earn the most money.

Suggestions for odd jobs for Candlemas

1 Shopping.
2 Washing up.
3 Cleaning shoes. (Don't forget to put newspaper on the

floor before you do this. Shoe polish over the floor might cost *you* 10p instead of earning 5p!)

4 Bed making.
5 Cleaning the inside of the car. (Don't offer to wash the car because it might be a freezing cold day – you don't want to get frost-bite!)
6 Taking the dog for a walk.
7 Promising not to tell awful jokes for at least an hour!

When all the jobs are done, count up how much money you have collected.

On February 2nd everyone gives the money to the teacher and waits to find out who has collected the most. If anyone has a spare candle at home it could be given to the teacher as well – in the interests of history!

SILENCE in the class as the teacher counts.

Then the boy and girl who have collected most money are declared King and Queen of Candlemas. (Of course, if you go to an all boys school there can only be a King, and there can only be a Queen at an all girls school!)

The King and Queen now rule until March 16th, and they can make one afternoon a week into playtime of one kind or another.

Suggestions for afternoon activities

1 Extra games.
2 Extra art lessons.
3 Story reading by the teacher.
4 Playing charades.
5 If the weather is fine – just playing in the playground.

The rulers' other power of forgiving punishments must be handled very carefully.

Good ideas

1 Let someone off *one* set of lines.
2 Dismiss just one detention class.
3 Let the whole class free from just one set of homework.

You must be careful with this because, if you take it too far, you won't be celebrating Candlemas next year.

At the end of the day, if the teacher does buy sweets and cakes with the collected money, perhaps he or she will let you eat them just before going home. Why don't you get the candles lit as well?

'The Fair Maid of February' is the snowdrop flower. There is an old rhyme that says:

The snowdrop in purest white array,
First rears her head on Candlemas Day.

Have you seen a snowdrop?

It was thought to be unlucky to bring snowdrops into the house before Candlemas Day. Even on February 2nd you couldn't take just one snowdrop into the house, because one snowdrop was supposed to be unlucky. So if you want to cheer up someone by giving them the first flowers of spring, make sure that you only pick snowdrops after February 2nd and that you give more than one. Another name for snow-drops is Candlemas Bells – but the most interesting thing I found out about the snowdrop was that it doesn't mean 'drop' of snow, it means drop as in eardrop – the old word for earring. So, why don't you pick four snowdrops, tie them together in twos and hang them over your ears as snow earrings?

February

You could also press some snowdrops for use later on in the month. Get a piece of blotting paper or tissue, put the snowdrops carefully on the paper, making the best shapes, then put more tissue paper on the top and put this between two heavy books. Leave them until February 13th when you can use them to decorate Valentine cards because . . .

February 14th is St Valentine's Day.

Valentine cards are supposed to be sent to the one you love – but they're not to be signed so you're kept guessing.
Why don't you make a Valentine card?

You need: A piece of white paper or thin card approximately 6 × 6 in (15 × 15 cm)
A piece of coloured paper approximately 4 × 4 in (10 × 10 cm)
A piece of white paper 3 × 3 in (8 × 8 cm)
Some pressed flowers
Scissors
Needle or pair of compasses
Glue

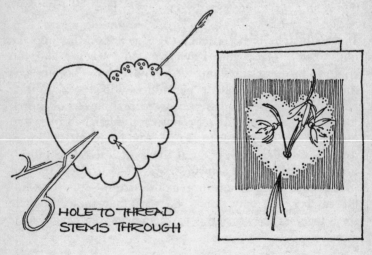

HOLE TO THREAD STEMS THROUGH

What to do :

1 Fold the piece of white card in half.
2 Stick the pressed flowers on the front.

OR

1 Fold the white card in half.
2 Cut a heart shape out of the white paper.
3 Decorate the edges by cutting curves and piercing each one with the needle or compass point.
4 Make a hole in the lower centre of the heart to thread the stems of the pressed flowers through.
5 Stick the snowdrops on the heart.
6 Stick the heart on the piece of coloured paper and then stick the coloured paper to the front of the card.

Don't forget – you must put more than one snowdrop on the card.

Messages

Here is an old message sent by the fourth Duke of Portland to Miss Betsy Keatts in 1847. Do you know what it says?

The answer is at the end of this chapter. Perhaps you could make up a message like it for the inside of your card.

> Knock, knock.
> Who's there?
> Snow.
> Snow who?
> Snow idea! Have you?

Valentine's Day is also the day when you are supposed to be able to find out the name of the person you're going to marry. There are lots of old ways of doing this, but the one I like best is this:

What to do:

1 Get a large bowl of water and put it in the garden the night before St Valentine's Day.
2 Cut up twenty-six pieces of paper and write the letters of the alphabet on them, using a biro.
3 Place the letters face down in the bowl of water.
4 Leave them in the garden and go to bed.
5 On Valentine's Day go into the garden – the breeze will have blown some of the pieces of paper over, and they will be the initials or the whole name of the person you are to marry.

Well, enough of this lovey dovey stuff! Now back to the rough stuff!

Did you know that football is a special game in February? Actually, it's a very special kind of football. A game with no rules. Shrove Tuesday usually comes in February because it is forty days before Easter. Those forty days of Lent are supposed to be a time of quietness and fasting. Shrove Tuesday (sometimes called Mischief Day) was the last day before Lent, so it was the last day for fun and food for a long time. In some villages and towns traffic would be stopped and all the men would come out into the streets at a set time. The church bell would ring and a football would be thrown into the crowd. Sometimes there would be teams – say one street against another, or one village against another, and in that case there would be goalposts at each end of the village, but in other places there were no teams; you just had to try to keep in control of the ball longer than anyone else. I saw a game of street football played once and everyone was madly rushing around, when, suddenly, someone kicked the

ball very hard. It went right into the next street and landed on the top of an open-topped bus and was never seen again. So in the playground on Shrove Tuesday it's No Rules Football. Just see how long one person can keep the ball, and declare a winner at the end.

> What football team do horses hate?
> Tottenham (HOT SPURS).

We can't leave February without knowing how to make pancakes. The games on Shrove Tuesday were the last fun before Lent, and pancake making was a way of using up extra food to make fasting easier in Lent. It was the last time that luxury foods could be used. All over Britain different Shrove Tuesday meals were made – sometimes it was broth (Scotland), or doughnuts (Hertfordshire), frying pan pudding (Lincolnshire) or pea soup (Cornwall) – but the most usual meal and the meal we still make today is pancakes.

As one of the main things in pancakes is eggs, why don't you ask if you can do another old custom before you make the pancake? It's called *egg shackling*.

You put eggs – as many as you're going to need in the pancakes – in a sieve and hold the sieve over a bowl. Each egg has the name of a member of your family on it and is then shaken, knocking the eggs about.

The owner of the last whole egg left is the winner.

The only messy thing about this is pulling the broken eggshells out of the sieve.

> Mummy, Mummy, will the pancakes be long?
> No, dear – *round!*

Pancakes

You need: Mixing bowl
Fork or whisk
Frying-pan
Fish slice

4 oz (125 g) flour
1 egg
Pinch of salt
½ pint (225 ml) milk
1 egg-cupful water
Small pat of butter
Caster sugar
Lemon juice

What to do: 1 Sieve the flour into a bowl.
2 Add the egg and pinch of salt. Mix together.
3 Add milk and water slowly (to stop lumps forming) and whisk together for about 5 minutes. The mixture should be bubbly and fluffy.
4 Put butter in frying-pan and melt slowly.
5 Pour in just enough mixture to cover the bottom of the frying-pan.
6 Cook on a low heat until it starts to thicken.
7 If you can, shake the pancake loose from the pan, then toss it up in the air, catch it in the pan and cook the other side. Good luck! Otherwise, turn the pancake over with a fish slice and cook the other side.
8 When cooked, put the pancake on a warm plate, sprinkle with caster sugar and lemon, roll up into a sausage and put somewhere to keep warm until you have made all the pancakes you need.

Eat the pancakes immediately and then shout:

> *Tippety, tippety tin,*
> *Give me a pancake and I'll come in.*
> *Tippety, tippety toe,*
> *Give me a pancake and then I'll go.*

(West Somerset rhyme)

Other things to do

Shrove Tuesday

Go to the top of a hill as the church bell strikes midday on Shrove Tuesday, put your ear to the ground and you should hear the witches frying their pancakes.

(Tollington, Beds.)

Ash Wednesday
(the day after Shrove Tuesday)

Carry a piece of twig from an ash tree in your pocket. Anybody at school who doesn't have an ash twig has to have his or her feet trodden on.

Kissing Friday
(the Friday after Ash Wednesday)

Every boy has the right to kiss any girl he wishes – but only one . . . so get your running shoes on, girls!

Answer to Valentine

> If you love I as I love you
> No knife shall cut our love in two.

March

Strong winds blow the man of March
As he climbs up the hill,
But he's happy to watch the grasses dance
With the yellow daffodil.

If you *have* to go out on March 1st, make sure you shut the door of your house as quickly as possible, for there is an old saying which goes:

> *On the first of March, the fleas start jumping.*
> [*or*]
> *If from fleas you would be free,*
> *On the 1st of March let all your doors and windows closed be.*

Mad March is marble and skipping time. All through Lent, the traditional games played are marbles and skipping. The games were stopped on the stroke of twelve noon on Good Friday, which in some places was called Marble Day or Long Rope Day. Why don't you start marble and skipping championships? There are lots of different games to play. You could have four games of marbles and four skipping games and play them until you find a champion of each game. Then have semi-finals between the winners, and finals to find the over-all winner. The winner of your group of finals could then take on the winner of other groups until on Good Friday the final of the championships is held. But don't forget the games must finish by twelve noon.

Marbles

Marbles can be bought at most toy shops and they come in different sizes. These sizes have differing names depending on which part of the country you live in. Here are a few names: Bosses, Bonzes, Aggies, Glassies, Alleys, Baries, Poppos, Stonies, Tiddlers, Taws, Commoneys, Maradiddles, Steelies, Tolleys.

The game of marbles has been played for hundreds of years and some historians say that it might have been started by rolling eggs – but that sounds a bit messy to me. In the past, round stones, hazelnuts, round balls of baked clay and even cherry stones have been used, so if marbles cost more than your pocket money will allow, be inventive – use something else.

Some games of marbles

The correct way to flick a marble

Taw

You can have any number of players in this game. A chalk circle is drawn on the ground and each player puts two marbles in the circle. Walk ten steps away from the circle and flick a marble towards it, trying to knock as many marbles as possible out of the circle. Every time a player flicks a marble out of the circle it is his and he collects it before the next player may play.

Should the marble that has been flicked fail to move any marbles out of the ring, then the player has to leave the marble he has just flicked in the circle as well. He can't get it back.

You find the winner by counting up how many marbles you have won!

Bombers

Again, any number of players can play this game. Draw a circle big enough to take two marbles from each player.

The rules are the same as in Taw except that the player

drops a marble from eye level straight on to the group of marbles in the circle to try and remove them.

Holeseys
(to be played outside)

Dig a shallow dish shape out of the earth. Each player puts five marbles into the dish shape.

Walk ten paces back.

Toss up or dibb up to choose who will start and, taking it in turns, flick one marble at a time trying to get it into the scooped-out bit. The first one to get a marble in wins all the marbles in the hole. (Nerve-wracking – and possibly instant loss of all marbles!)

Boss Out
(for two players)

One player flicks a marble any distance he wants and it then becomes the target. The other player tries to hit the first marble. If he does he wins both marbles. If he doesn't, the other player wins them. This game continues with the players taking it in turns to start until one person has run out of marbles.

Perhaps you can think of many more games, or perhaps you have slightly different rules to the same games. Let the championship commence, and don't stop until Good Friday.

Skipping

Funnily enough, skipping used to be a game that boys were better at than girls. Nowadays it seems to be the other way round.

Suggested skipping games

1 Counting to see how many times a person can skip over a rope by jumping with both feet together.
2 Counting again, but this time hopping from foot to foot in turn.
3 Skipping by hopping on one foot only.

For the championships, you could get all the skippers who have come through to the finals and make them skip whichever way they please, but it has to be in time to clapping. The clapping is done by the people who didn't get into the finals. Start by clapping very slowly and as the contestants start to get tired, clap faster and faster. The exhausted but surviving skipper is the winner of the contest.

Throughout the year, many strange customs take place, some for religious reasons, some for fun and some, apparently, for no reason at all.

Every year on March 25th in the village of Tichborne in Hampshire, the priest of the church can be seen blessing a ton and a half of flour and then giving it away in bags, pillow cases and sacks to the villagers of Tichborne, Cheriton and Lane End. Here's the reason why.

Story Time

In the twelfth century, that's over seven hundred years ago, there lived a very kind and generous woman called Lady Maybella. It was the custom in those days that if a woman had a lot of money, it all belonged to her husband from the day of the marriage. So although Lady Maybella had been very rich, she had to ask her husband, Sir Roger de Tichborne, for anything she wanted.

Sir Roger was not the nicest of people, so Lady Maybella had to beg him for everything. Most of the things she had she gave to the poor. When she was very ill and dying, she asked her husband if he would still be kind to the poor people after she was dead. She wanted him to give bread to the poor once a year. Sir Roger wasn't happy about this, for he would have to give up some of the flour that he made from the wheat he grew and he didn't like to give anything away for nothing! So he decided to set Lady Maybella a difficult task and if she could do it then he would give flour for the bread to the poor. Now, remember that Lady Maybella was very ill! Sir Roger took a burning log from the fire and said that however much of his land Lady Maybella could get round before the flames from the log went out, he would set aside for the growing of wheat and this wheat would be made into flour for the poor.

Lady Maybella called to her maids and they lifted her from her bed into the grounds outside. Now, everyone knows that March is a very windy month, but as Sir Roger carried the burning log outside to watch Lady Maybella, the winds dropped and the flames from the log burned brightly with an unflickering flame. Lady Maybella tried to stand up but she was too weak, so she began to crawl on her hands and knees. As she disappeared in the distance, the servants held their breath and watched the flames on the log. Sir Roger was getting more and more angry as he saw how far his wife was crawling – he thought he had set her an impossible task. He saw Lady Maybella turn and start to crawl across the land – then, still crawling, she turned again, this time to crawl down back to the house. All the time the flames burned brightly.

As Lady Maybella was nearing the house, the log was nearly all burned, and when at last she reached the place where she had started, the flame suddenly went out. She had crawled over an area of *twenty-three* acres! These twenty-three acres are, even today, still known as the 'Crawls'.

Before Lady Maybella died, she made Sir Roger promise to give all the flour grown on the 'Crawls' to the poor every March 25th, and, just to make sure he kept his promise, she put a curse on the Tichborne family and house. The curse said that anyone in the family not giving flour to the poor on March 25th would find that the house would collapse, their money would be lost and seven sons would be born followed by seven daughters and the name of Tichborne would die out.

The flour was given every year until 1796, when Sir Henry Tichborne gave money to the church instead of flour to the people. He had seven sons, his eldest son had seven daughters and half the family house fell down, so a very worried son of Sir Henry, a Sir Edward Doughty-Tichborne, started up the custom again – and things have been all right ever since. Strange story, isn't it?

Why don't you try to crawl as far as you can on March 25th? You could do it as a competition with some friends – but I bet you won't crawl as far as Lady Maybella!

Another day to do with ladies is in March. It's the fourth Sunday of Lent, which is Mother's Day.

> 'Mummy, Mummy, why do I keep going
>   round in circles?'
> 'Shut up – or I'll tie your other foot to the
>   floor!'

A long time ago, Mother's Day (or Mothering Sunday) was a day when apprentices and servants were given the day off to visit their mothers and so they would take presents as well. Nowadays, it seems to be just another reason for spending hard-earned pocket money! So, why don't you *make* a present and card?

Cards

1 Get out an old Christmas card from your secret hiding place. Find one with a good picture on it and cut off the old message. Write a new message on the back of the picture.

2 If you've got some spare cardboard or paper in your secret hiding place, you could fold it into a card shape and draw your own picture.

March is the time when violets are in bloom and these were often the flowers given on Mother's Day. Perhaps you could draw a picture of some violets or press some in the same way that you pressed snowdrops. If you haven't any flowers you can still make a card.

You need: Mauve tissue, toilet paper or crepe paper
                 Thick white paper or thin card
                 Scissors
                 Coloured pencils
                 Glue

What to do: 1 Cut petal shapes from the mauve tissue.

2 Fold the paper into a card shape and draw a pattern of green leaves and stems on the front leaving spaces for the flowers.

3 Put a spot of glue in each flower space and stick five petals there as shown.

4 Cut some very small triangles from white paper and stick one in the centre of each violet. Draw a yellow dot in the middle and your violet is complete.

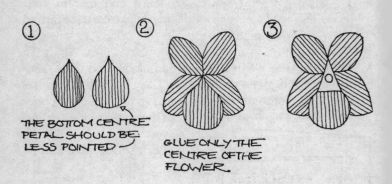

THE BOTTOM CENTRE PETAL SHOULD BE LESS POINTED

GLUE ONLY THE CENTRE OF THE FLOWER.

Presents

Peg Dolls

You need:

Pegs – the old fashioned wooden ones (If no one has any to give you, they cost very little in the shops.)
Biro and red crayon
Glue
Cotton wool
A white paper doily
Blue or black paper

What to do:

1 Using a biro, draw the doll's face and shoes on the peg. A red crayon will colour the cheeks.

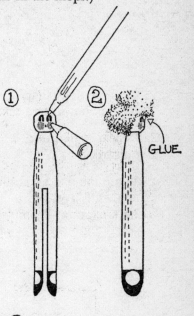

2 Glue a small ball of cotton wool on to the head and shape it into a hairstyle.

3 Cut the white doily in half and then cut one half to the shape shown.

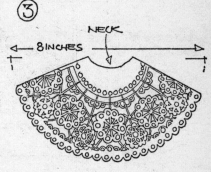

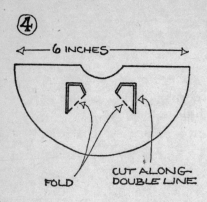

④

◄— 6 INCHES —►

FOLD

CUT ALONG
DOUBLE LINE

4 Cut the dark paper into a half circle 6 in (15 cm) in diameter. Cut the neck as shown and then carefully cut the shapes for the arms and fold them forwards. (It is easiest to do the cutting with a craft knife, so get an adult to help you.)

5 Glue the doily shape round the neck of the doll, sticking the join down the back.

6 Repeat steps 4 and 5 with the dark paper to make the overdress.

7 Finish the doll by cutting shapes as shown to make the cap, cuffs and collar. A small bow shape cut from the dark paper will complete the cap.

⑤

JOIN
AT
BACK

⑥

⑦

This doll is easy to make and can stand up on her own. Make several of these dolls and hide them away in your secret place. You'll find out why later.

Scented Bag

You know all those bits of soap that get left over from a large tablet of soap – the bits that are too small to use and usually get lost in the bath? Well, here's a way of using them up.

1 Collect all the small pieces of soap you can find, especially the nice smelling ones.

2 Get a pretty handkerchief, or a square of material, but make sure no one needs them.

3 Put the soap in the centre of the handkerchief or material and twist the cloth round until it looks like this:

Then tie a ribbon or length of coloured wool round the material above the soap and bingo! It's finished.

Your mother can now put this in her wardrobe or chest of drawers and it will make her clothes smell good.

Don't forget. Make more than one and keep them till later.

Make a Cake

Mothering Sunday used to be the day when people would make Simnel cakes to give their mothers. Nobody really knows how we got the word Simnel; there are all sorts of explanations. Here's the one I like best.

A brother and sister were making a cake for their mother when they began to argue. One said the cake should be baked – the other said it should be boiled. So they divided the mixture in half and one half was boiled and the other was baked. Then the two halves were put together. The brother was called Simon and the sister was Nelly – so the cake was called Sim-nel. (But I suppose it could have been called Nel-sim.)

Here's a recipe for an easy sponge cake that someone could perhaps help you with.

You need: Two 7 in (18 cm) sponge tins
Mixing bowl

A little butter or margarine
3 eggs
4 oz (100 g) caster sugar
4 oz (100 g) self-raising flour
Strawberry jam
12 sweets such as chocolate buttons

What to do: 1 Turn the oven on to gas No. 4 or 350 °F (180 °C) electric.

2 Grease the sponge tins with a little butter or margarine until the inside is slightly greasy. Don't use too much.

3 Mix the eggs and sugar in a bowl for about six minutes. (Remember to crack the eggs first and throw away the shells – this is not eggshell cake!)

4 Sieve the flour into the mixture of eggs and sugar and then gently mix the flour in until it is all creamy and smooth.

5 Put half the mixture in one tin and half in the other.

6 Put the tins in the oven near the top for 20 minutes or until the cakes are light golden brown.

7 Take out of the oven (with oven gloves or a cloth) and leave them to cool.

8 When cool, turn the first sponge out on to a plate. Cover the sponge with strawberry jam or any jam you like.

9 Now turn out the next sponge making sure the best side stays up, and put the sponge on top of the jam.

10 All you need to do now is to sprinkle sugar on top of the cake and decorate it with twelve sweets – one for each month of the year, or one for each of Jesus's Apostles.

Q. Why is there a Mother's Day, a Father's Day but not a Son's Day?

A. But there is – there's a Sunday every week!

April

Birds come in from across the sea,
And the gardens begin to flower,
But the April man still watches out
For a sudden rainy shower.

April begins with All Fools Day on April 1st. This is the day when people are allowed to play tricks on other people. My favourite April Fool was to take my mother and father an early morning cup of tea, but instead of putting sugar in the tea, I put salt. I remember rolling about with laughter as my mum and dad pulled awful faces. But . . . have a proper cup of tea waiting outside to avoid awful consequences!

When I was older, I used to work on Saturdays in a hairdresser's – and I was caught out. I was told to go to the butcher's to get twelve fly's legs to make into false eyelashes. The butcher and the hairdresser thought it was very funny but I felt an idiot!

The trouble with April Fool's Day is trying to find something to do that no one else has done before – then you can really catch people out. But don't forget that any April Fool that is played after twelve midday means that the joke is on you.

> *April Fool's past and gone,*
> *You're the fool and I am none.*

On April 6th there used to be Candle Auctions. A candle was lit and a pin stuck in it about 1 in (2½ cm) from the top.

Then people would start bidding for a piece of church land to be let to the poor people for a year. The person bidding when the candle burned down enough to let the pin fall became the owner of the land.

Now, this custom doesn't go on a lot nowadays, but why don't you hold a sort of candle auction of your own in your family?

Ask if you can have a candle on the table at tea time. Get one of your parents to stick a pin in it a little way below the top and then light it. Everyone at the table has to keep counting in turns, for example, Dad says 'one', and you say 'two', Mum says 'three' and so on until the pin falls out of the candle – and whoever has just spoken has to do the . . . *washing up!*

BOY: Will you join me in the washing up?
DAD: Sorry son, the bowl's too small!

Easter usually comes in the month of April. It is what is called a 'moveable feast' because the date of it is fixed according to the moon. Easter Sunday has to be the first Sunday after the full moon which can be on or after the 21st of March! PHEW! If you can understand that, then you can understand why all the days that concern Lent cannot be given a definite date. Lent is a period of time before Easter and if Easter falls on different dates, so will Lent.

Anyway, *whenever* Easter is it's usually a time that has a lot of things to do in it. It starts with Good Friday, and don't forget it's the day to end the skipping and marbles championships.

Good Friday is also the traditional day to give and eat hot cross buns. People selling hot cross buns would shout:

> *Hot Cross Buns,*
> *Hot Cross Buns,*
> *One a penny, two a penny,*
> *Hot Cross Buns.*
> *If you have no daughters*
> *Give them to your sons.*
> *One a penny, two a penny,*
> *Hot Cross Buns.*

It would be nice if you could make some hot cross buns (or get someone to help you make them). Take them round to your friends as a present, calling out the rhyme as you go. Here's a recipe.

Hot Cross Buns

You may need a bit of help with making these – but it's worth it!

You need: Large mixing bowl
Smaller bowl
Baking tray
Small saucepan

1 lb (450 g) flour
1 teaspoonful salt
1 teaspoonful mixed spice
2 oz (60 g) butter
2 oz (60 g) currants
1 oz (30 g) yeast
1½ oz (45 g) sugar
½ pint (250 ml) milk

What to do: 1 Turn on the oven to gas No. 7 or 425° F
(220° C) electric.

2 Mix the flour, salt and spice in a bowl.

3 Rub in the butter.

4 Add the currants and put the mixture in a
warm place for a while.

5 Mix the yeast and sugar together gently in a
separate bowl and leave for a few minutes
until frothy.

6 Add the yeast mixture and milk to the flour
mixture. This should look like a fluffy
dough.

7 Beat the mixture for about 5 minutes.
Cover with a cloth and leave in a warm
place for an hour. (The dough 'rises' up so
make sure you are using a big bowl.)

8 When the dough has risen, turn it out on
to a floured surface and knead it. (That
means keep folding it over and pressing it
with your hands. This bit is lovely and
messy.)

9 Cut the dough into twelve portions and roll
each portion into a round ball.

10 Put each ball on a floured baking tray and make a cross by using the back of a knife and pressing quite deeply.

11 Put in a warm place for 20 minutes. This will make the buns rise again – so make sure they are not too close together.

12 Bake in the hot oven for about 20 minutes.

13 Warm a little more milk with some sugar in a small saucepan.

14 Brush the milk and sugar mixture over the buns after you've taken them out of the oven. This gives them that lovely shiny, sticky look.

15 When the buns have cooled down a bit, hand them round.

Hot cross buns baked on Good Friday were supposed to have magic powers. It is said that you could keep a hot cross bun which had been made on Good Friday for at least a year and it wouldn't go mouldy.

Hardened old hot cross buns were supposed to protect the house from fire.

Sailors took them to sea with them to prevent shipwreck.

A bun baked on Good Friday and left to get hard could be grated up and put in some warm milk and this was supposed to stop an upset tummy. It sounds as if it would taste a lot nicer than most tummy medicines – but I don't think I'll try it – it might make me worse, especially if the hot cross bun has been hanging around for a year.

Q. What's the difference between a riddle and some children sitting on a bun?

A. One is a conundrum and the other is a bun under 'em!

The people of Exmoor believed that flowers planted at midday on Good Friday should have double flowers. But whereever you go in Britain, it is supposed to be very lucky to plant potatoes on this day because the Devil is said to have no power over the Earth on Good Friday. So help Dad or Mum in the garden today.

Easter wouldn't be Easter without *eggs*. But do you know why we have Easter eggs? After Pancake Day on Shrove Tuesday, eggs were not supposed to be eaten until Easter. But all through Lent the hens would go on laying, and the eggs wouldn't be eaten – so they would be saved up and by Easter there would be loads of them. That's one reason. Another is that because Easter comes at the beginning of spring when all the plants are starting to grow, the new lambs are being born and the whole world seems to be waking up, the egg is used as a symbol for spring. It is the sign of birth.

Nowadays, Easter eggs are made from chocolate or frosted sugar but that's only a recent thing. Ordinary chicken's or duck's eggs were decorated for Easter in times gone by.

Here are some ways of decorating eggs for breakfast.

Before the eggs are boiled:

1 Put icing sugar dyes in the water that the eggs are to be boiled in. Cochineal, for instance, will give you pink, orange or red eggs, depending on the colour of the egg and how much cochineal you put in.
2 Put gorse or wild broom flowers in the water to make the eggs bright yellow, or spinach leaves for green eggs.
3 Cover the eggs with onion skins. Secure them with elastic bands or string in a criss-cross pattern and boil them. This will make a marbled egg of brownish colours.

After the eggs have been boiled:

1 When the eggs have cooled down a little, crayon with wax crayons all over them, using as many colours as you like. Then, with the wrong end of a spoon or something pointed, gently scratch away some of the wax, either to make a pattern or a picture, or to spell out someone's name.

2 Again, when the eggs have cooled, you could paint pictures on them with water colours or pencils. You could also put a coloured ribbon round the egg – use some from your secret drawer.

An Egg as a Present for Ever

Now this is very tricky but well worth doing and you have to be careful. If you're going to give an egg as something to last for ever, you must remember that eggs go off and when they do . . . phew! So the white and the yolk of the egg have to be removed. Now, this is fascinating and could be messy so don't hold the egg too hard!

You need: An egg
     A pin
     Paints or felt pens
     Varnish

What to do: 1 Make a small pin hole in one end of the egg.
    2 Make a pin hole in the other end and wiggle the pin about to make a slightly bigger hole.
    3 Hold the egg up and poke about with the pin so that you can burst the yolk. You'll know when you've done this because there will be yellow on the pin.
    4 Shake the egg a bit – this makes it easier to remove the insides.
    5 Now for the fun . . . Get a bowl and put your mouth over the end of the egg with the small hole in it and blow, catching the insides in the bowl. Every now and again, if the egg gets stuck, shake it. It only takes about two minutes to empty the egg.
    6 Now you have to wash out the inside of the egg because even a tiny bit of stale egg can pong something shocking!
     There are two ways of washing the egg out. Go to the sink and put the tap on so that a small stream of water comes out. Let this pour gently into the larger hole of the egg

and fill the eggshell up with water. Then blow the water out.

The second method – and I prefer this – is to fill your mouth up with water and blow the water into the egg. It comes swishing out the other end like a water pistol – great fun! When the water that comes out of the egg is the same colour as the water that went in, then the eggshell is clean.

7 Dry the eggshell gently, then paint the egg with either nail varnish or enamel paint (the type you use for model aeroplanes). You could also paint with water colours or felt tips. Let the egg dry and then varnish it all over. The varnishing makes the egg stronger, but you don't have to varnish when you use enamel paint. Make sure you put newspaper down before you start painting!

8 If you aren't too good at painting pretty scenes or patterns, you could just paint the egg one colour and then stick on silver and gold stars or any design you like.

Don't just make one egg like this. If you are allowed the eggs, make a few. Give some as Easter gifts and wrap the others in tissue paper or toilet roll. Put them in a box so that they won't break and put them away in your secret hiding place. I'll tell you why later!

An Egg-shaped Gift Box

You need: An egg
String or elastic bands
Face cream or margarine
Paste
Newspaper or coloured paper
Paints
Tissue paper

What to do: 1 Hard-boil the egg.
  2 When cold, put an elastic band or a piece

of string round it either from top to bottom
or round the middle.

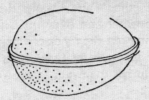

3 Gently rub a little face cream or margarine
over the surface of the egg to form a barrier
against the glue.
4 Mix up some wallpaper paste or some flour
and water.
5 Cut up newspaper or thin coloured paper
into small pieces about ¼ in (5 mm) square.
6 Using the paste, stick the pieces of paper
over the egg up to, but not over, the elastic
band. Then repeat with a second layer.
7 When the egg is dry the paper covering can
simply be pulled off and painted. (You
won't need to paint it if you've used coloured
paper.) When the paint has dried, you can
line one half with coloured tissue or toilet
paper and put a sweet or a small present
inside.

Make lots of these gift boxes and put them away in your
secret place. I'll tell you why later!

A custom that happens in some places on Easter Monday is
called Egg Rolling. Why don't you and your family or friends
do it where you live?

You each have a hard-boiled egg with your name on it. Go
out for a walk and find the nearest grassy slope. Even parks
have hilly bits. Then roll the eggs down the hill. The one
that rolls the furthest is the winner!

> Q. What goes over the water, under the water, on
>   the water and yet doesn't touch the water?
> A. An egg in a duck's tummy.

April 23rd is St George's Day. St George was the patron
saint of England and it is said that he once saved a village
from a great danger. The village was frightened of a large,
fierce dragon who lived close by, so St George killed the
dragon.

Why don't you make a dragon puppet for St George's Day?

You need: A piece of thick paper about 6 in × 2 in (15
             cm × 5 cm)
             Coloured pens
             Scissors
             Eight empty cotton reels
             Thick string
             Crepe paper
             Cotton
             A stick about 2 ft (60 cm) long

What to do: 1 Fold the paper in half.
2 Draw a dragon's face up to the fold in the paper.

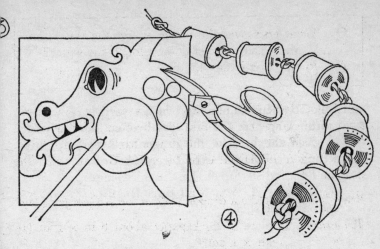

3 Cut around the face, being careful not to
cut through the fold in the paper. Open the
paper out and colour both sides of the face.

4 Thread thick string through the cotton
reels, tying a large knot between each one.

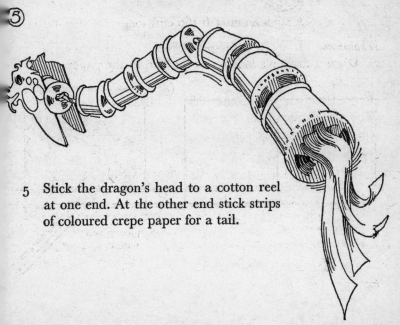

5 Stick the dragon's head to a cotton reel
at one end. At the other end stick strips
of coloured crepe paper for a tail.

6 Cut three lengths of cotton each 1 yard (1 metre) long. Tie the first length of cotton between the head of the dragon and the second reel. Tie the second length between the fifth and sixth reel. Tie the third length to the last reel. Attach all three lengths of cotton to the stick.

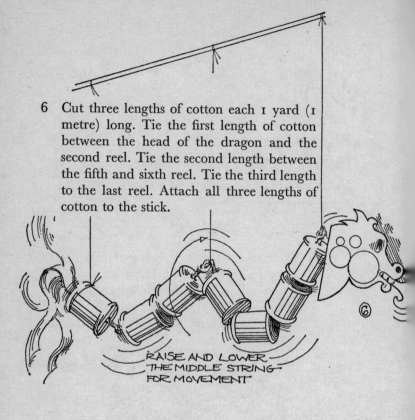

RAISE AND LOWER THE MIDDLE STRING FOR MOVEMENT

Every time you wiggle the stick, the dragon slithers about. You could also paint the cotton reel red and white (the colours of St George's flag).

Don't forget to make more than one – and put the others away in your secret drawer. You'll find out why later.

May

Children play beneath a tree
That's covered with flowering cherry;
The sun peeps out from behind a cloud
To make the May man merry.

May

So many things happen in May. It seems to be a happy month when the year starts to wake up and get busy.

First thing in the morning on May 1st, young girls used to rush out into the garden to wash their faces in the May dew. There is an old tale that says that May dew has magic properties and that anyone who has washed their face in it will have a beautiful complexion all through the year. This dew was also supposed to be able to remove freckles – but I think they're rather nice and I've never understood why people should want to get rid of them. May dew is also supposed to get rid of spots and pimples – and anything that can help do that must be good.

Why don't you try to collect some May dew?

You need: An alarm clock to get you up early
Large pad of cotton wool
Jug
Small clean bottles with lids or stoppers
Labels
Permission to go out
    (maybe your mum will go with you)

What to do: 1   When you've got up and are dressed warmly (for it is quite cold early in the morning), go to the nearest place that has any grass. This could be your garden or a park.

2   The dew collects on the blades of grass, so if you wipe the grass with the cotton wool, the cotton wool will get soaking wet.

3   Squeeze out the dew from the cotton wool into the jug.

4   Repeat over and over again until you have got enough dew.

5   When you return home you could use some

of the dew to wash your face and fill the
bottles with the rest of the dew.

6 Put a label on each bottle. Give one bottle
to your mum and put the rest away safely –
till later.

A maid who on the first of May
Goes to the fields at break of day
And washes in the dew from the hawthorn tree,
Will ever after handsome be.

In some parts of Britain, May 1st
is called Garland Day.

The first of May is Garland Day,
So please remember the garland.
We don't come here but once a year,
So please remember the garland.

May garlands are very easy to make. Sometimes they are
just a bunch of pretty spring flowers tied on the top of a
stick with ribbons hanging down.

Other types of garlands used to have May dolls in them as
well. This was just a small doll, prettily dressed, which was
either attached to the posy of flowers like the one above, or
suspended in the middle of two decorated hoops. You could
make the hoops by bending wire coat-hangers, but do get
some help with this.

One hoop is pushed inside another, and each hoop is decorated with green leaves and flowers. A stick can be put straight down the middle and the doll attached to it. (You could make one of your peg dolls for this.) Anything else that will add to the decoration like ribbons or bells just makes it even prettier. If you make some of these they can hang in your classroom to make the day look festive, or take them round to your neighbours' houses to show them what you've done.

If you have any of those large hoops at school, perhaps you'd like to ask if you could use them to play an old May Day game.

The hoops are decorated with greenery and flowers. Then a long rope is passed through them and the two ends are tied to trees or posts in the playground. The game is to see how many balls you can throw through the hoops.

I'm sure one of your teachers will help you to tie the rope to somewhere high enough for you to enjoy the game properly. You could make it a team game. Each hoop could use flowers or ribbons of just one colour. You could have a white hoop, a yellow hoop, a blue hoop and a green hoop. Dividing the class into four, you could see how many balls you can throw through your own hoop in, say, five minutes. The winning team could choose who is to be the May Queen.

May

When I was at school, the way we chose the May Queen was
quite easy really. Instead of staring rudely at all the girls, the
queen was decided by a competition. On May 1st all the girls
came to school wearing a May crown. All the crowns were
taken off and left in a classroom on a table. The teacher
would then pick his or her favourite and walk out to the
playground with it where we were waiting. The owner of
the crown was the May Queen for the day and the rest of the
girls were her attendants.

Here's how I made my May crown.

You need: Two strips of thick paper
Glue
Blu-Tack
Flowers
Ferns
Ribbons

What to do:

1 Cut two strips of thick paper about 2 in
(5 cm) wide and 2 ft (60 cm) long.

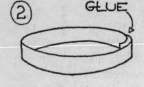

2 Put one strip around your head
and fold one end over the other
until it fits nicely. Carefully
remove it from your head holding the two ends together and
then glue them. If the ends keep
springing apart, you can keep
them together with a paper clip
or a dressmaker's pin.

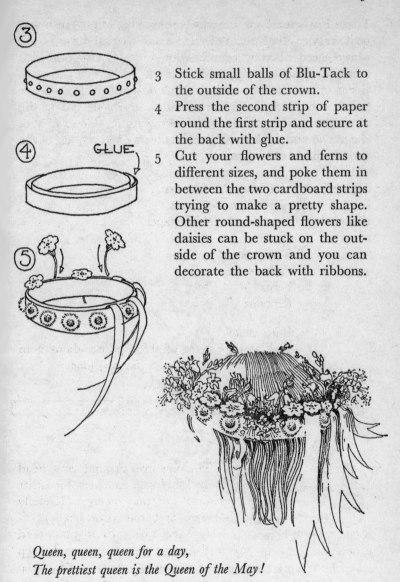

3 Stick small balls of Blu-Tack to the outside of the crown.

4 Press the second strip of paper round the first strip and secure at the back with glue.

5 Cut your flowers and ferns to different sizes, and poke them in between the two cardboard strips trying to make a pretty shape. Other round-shaped flowers like daisies can be stuck on the outside of the crown and you can decorate the back with ribbons.

Queen, queen, queen for a day,
The prettiest queen is the Queen of the May!

Perhaps you can think of other ways of making a May crown.

There is a special costume for the boys on May Day too. As well as a May Queen at your school, why don't you have a 'Jack in the Green'? Jack in the Green is supposed to be Summer itself, and as summer is a time when everything is green and growing, Jack is covered in green. So choose a boy to be King of the Summer or Jack in the Green and cover him from head to knees in greenery – ribbons, branches, ferns, etc. Leave enough room for his eyes to peep through so he looks like a walking bush.

Jack in the Green can stand with the May Queen. If you have a netball post in your playground you can pretend that it is a maypole, and the May Queen and Jack in the Green can stand by it while the rest of the class dance round them in a circle. You could even get some of your garlands hung around the top of the netball post to make it look more authentic.

I say, I say, I say. Who always goes to bed with his shoes on?

I dunno, I dunno, I dunno. Who does go to bed with his shoes on?

A horse, of course!

Hobby Horses

In some parts of the country, men or children dress up in hobby horse costumes on May 1st every year. The hobby horse dances through the streets of the villages to welcome in the summer and to say goodbye to the winter. The horse jumps up high to greet the sun which will help the crops to grow and almost falls to the ground lying still, in remembrance of the cold, inactive ground of winter. Dancing with the hobby horse are many other people, some banging drums, some singing, and one man in particular who strokes the horse when he's lying down, looking after him as if to say 'Summer's nearly here.'

The Hobby Horse at Padstow in Cornwall is a lovely shape. It looks like this:

As you can see, the man carries the weight of the hobby horse on his shoulders. He has to be pretty fit too, as he dances from ten o'clock in the morning until ten at night.

An Easy Hobby Horse

If you have an old toy hobby horse, the type with wheels on that little ones play with, just put a hole in a large piece of fabric; an old sheet or tablecloth will do, if you can persuade someone to let you have it. Put the stick through the hole in the cloth and pull it up under the neck of the horse. Tie it on with a piece of string. Cut a peep hole in the front. Climb under the cloth and hold the stick, moving the cloth until you can see out of the peep hole. Now you can dance up and down.

If you haven't got a toy hobby horse, borrow a broom, turn it upside down and cover the brush with a duster. Tie two corners to form the ears. Draw and cut two eyes out of paper and stick them on to the broom with Blu-Tack. Now you can use this in the same way as the previous hobby horse.

When you've gathered your band of friends with you, you can shout, 'Oss, oss, wee oss', bang on the drum and dance around outside, stopping to bow kindly to anyone you meet to bring them good luck.

What game do horses like playing best?
Stable tennis!

May 13th is also a Garland Day like May 1st, but in Abbotsbury in Dorset it used to have a special, extra meaning. Abbotsbury was a fishing village, and May 13th, or Garland Day, marked the beginning of the fishing season. Beautifully made posies or garlands were put on the fishing boats to bring them good luck, and as the boats went out to sea, the garlands were thrown overboard as if they were a present to the sea. It must have been a super sight as the fishing boats floated in a sea of garlands and posies. Why don't you paint a picture of the scene?

Whitsuntide comes in May. It starts with Whit Sunday, which is always the seventh Sunday after Easter Sunday.

In Gloucestershire, Whit Sunday is called 'Bread and Cheese Day' because of a very strange custom. After the evening service in the church at St Briavels, small pieces of bread and cheese are thrown from a high stone wall to the people waiting below and everyone scrambles for some. It is said that this custom *has* to be performed otherwise the people of St Briavels will lose their grazing and timber privileges in the local wood.

Why don't you make yourself a toasted cheese sandwich on this day?

You need: Two slices of bread
Butter
Grated or sliced cheese
Chutney or tomato sauce

What to do: 1 Butter both pieces of bread.
2 Put the cheese on one slice.
3 Add a little chutney or tomato sauce – or an onion slice if you like it. (I like a slice of apple.)
4 Put the other slice of bread (buttered side next to the cheese) on top and press down.
5 Switch the grill on.
6 Put the sandwich under the grill and wait until the bread has turned a good shade of brown.

7   Using an oven cloth, turn the sandwich over and toast the other side.

8   When brown, switch off the grill and wait for the sandwich to cool a little.

9   When cool, put the sandwich on a plate, cut it in half and . . . eat it!

While we're on the subject of food, Whit Monday in Essex is the day when a large piece of bacon (a flitch) is given as a prize to a husband and wife who can prove that they have never quarrelled or never wished themselves single again. The name of this ceremony is the Dunmow Flitch Trial.

I should think that most of you aren't married yet – so why don't you give a ham sandwich to the one of your friends who has been the nicest person to be with throughout the year?

Q.   How many sexes are there?
A.   Three . . . female sex, male sex and insects!!

OH DEAR!   OH DEAR!   OH DEAR!

May 29th is special for two reasons. First of all, it is Oak Apple Day, and secondly, it is Arbor Tree Day.

Oak Apple Day

This is the day that people wear oak apples or oak leaves pinned to them to remember that on May 29th King Charles II returned triumphantly to London after the Restoration in 1660. The reason for the wearing of oak apples or oak leaves was to celebrate the King's narrow escape from capture by Cromwell's soldiers by hiding in an oak tree.

You could wear an oak leaf on May 29th. An oak leaf looks like this:

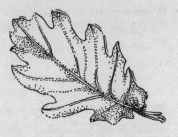

Or perhaps you would like to decorate your house with oak twigs and branches. You could paint some of the oak leaves that you have with gold paint and when they are dry put them away in your secret hiding place. I'll tell you why later!

Arbor Tree Day

In Aston on Clun in Shropshire, a large tree standing in the centre of the village is decorated with flags and the flags stay on the tree until the following May 29th. People say that in 1786 the Lord of the Manor got married on May 29th and the villagers decorated the tree with flags to celebrate the wedding. The bride was so pleased that she gave money to the village to allow the custom to continue. Although this is a super story, other people say that the villagers always decorated the tree because it would be a lovely, jolly day to marry but, whatever is true, the Lady certainly did give some money towards the custom.

Why don't you make some paper flags and hang them on a tree or bush on that day and see how long they stay there?

Q. Why did the King of France wear yellow braces on the first of May?
A. To keep his trousers up!

June

In June the man walks with his dog
Among tall corn and flowers,
And sits a while, and chats a while
To pass away the hours.

'June is busting out all over' with flowers and blossoms everywhere. Do you remember how we pressed some flowers in March? There are many more flowers about in June, so why don't you make a flower picture by pressing some more flowers? If you haven't got a garden and you don't live near the country where there are wild flowers, you could always buy a small bunch of flowers from the flower shop or ask the people in the shop if they have any odd flowers that they can't make into bunches. Tell them you want to press them and perhaps you'll get them a bit cheaper.

Word of warning: Always make sure you have permission to pick flowers, even in the countryside, and make sure you don't pull up the root. Just take off one or two flowers!

Collect some grasses too. When you have got your flowers and grasses, press them as you did in February and leave them to dry out.

1   When the flowers and grasses are properly pressed, you can arrange them on different shaped pieces of card to make pictures.

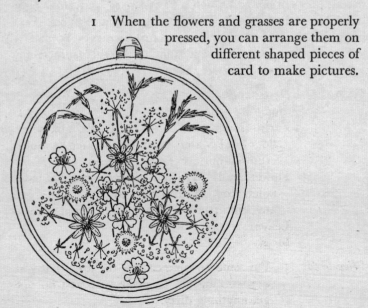

2 When you have made an arrangement you like, stick the flowers on to the card using a tiny spot of glue.

3 Then carefully varnish over the whole card. (I find colourless nail varnish the best.)

4 Leave until dry.

5 Glue a loop of ribbon on the back. This will allow you to hang the picture on your bed-room wall.

6 Make lots of these cards and put them away in your secret place. You'll find out why later.

At different times during June there are ceremonies called 'well dressings'. Springs and wells of fresh water that come from underground streams have always seemed to be magical things, so some wells are honoured with decorations. The decorations consist of branches of greenery and amazingly beautiful pictures made of flower petals and moss. Perhaps you would like to make a picture like this. It takes a long time, so only make a small picture. It will last for quite a few days and will look very nice.

You need: Newspaper
Small old saucer or plate
Earth (If you can't get any earth, mix some flour and water together, making it quite crumbly but also fairly damp.)
Flower petals – try to get only the ones that have fallen from the flowers and if you can't get any, cut up coloured paper into petal shapes.
Leaves
Moss

What to do: 1 Put some newspaper over the area that you are working on, to make sure you do not get anything dirty.

2 Put some damp earth or the flour and water mixture into the saucer or plate and press all over with the palm of your hand, until you have a smooth surface.

3 Now the flower petals. Arrange them in a pattern so that they overlap each other on the earth and press gently. Add the leaves and moss.

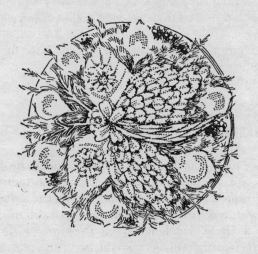

When you have finished your picture, perhaps you could put it by the bath or on a window-sill in the bathroom to celebrate all those lovely baths you can't wait to have!

What is frozen water?	Ice.
What is frozen cream?	Ice cream.
What is frozen tea?	Iced tea.
What is frozen ink?	Iced ink.

Well, have a bath then!

The longest day of the year is June 21st. In fact, it is so long that in some northern parts of Britain it hardly gets dark at all, just a sort of twilight. In Wiltshire there is a circle of huge stones at a place called Stonehenge, and hundreds of people go there to watch the sun rise on June 21st. These stones have stood in Wiltshire for thousands of years and no one knows how they got there. They must have been taken to the area, for this kind of stone is not naturally found there, but they are far too big to carry without a crane or a vast lorry – and there were no cranes or lorries all those years ago.

Here is my favourite story about how the stones got to Stonehenge.

Story Time

One night, the devil had nothing to do, so he decided to play a joke on the people who lived near Salisbury Plain in Wiltshire. He flew to Ireland and picked up some enormous stones and carried each one back to Salisbury, placing them in a circle. He laughed all the time as he thought how surprised the villagers would be in the morning when they saw the huge stones, standing there as if they had grown out of the earth during the night. But, as the devil worked, he hadn't noticed that a friar from a nearby monastery was hiding in a ditch and listening to him.

As the devil chuckled again and said, 'They'll never know how it was done,' the friar could not resist saying, 'That's what you think.' The devil heard what the friar said, he dropped the stone he was carrying into a stream where it can be seen now, and then he threw another stone at the friar. But as the friar was running so fast, it only banged him on the heel. To this day, that stone, which is known as the

Heel Stone, still stands away from the other stones, near the road. Good story, isn't it?

The middle of summer comes after the longest day and it is a time associated with witches, magic, fairies and dancing.

On the eve of Midsummer's Day, many bonfires used to be burnt all over the country. This was in praise of the sun, for the days were getting shorter and the sun appeared to be getting weaker, so people would light fires to try to strengthen the sun.

Midsummer's Eve, June 23rd, is a day when you can do so many things. As soon as it starts to get dark you can light torches – the battery ones not the fire ones – and dance round in a circle. You don't have to do this outside. Perhaps you could have a Midsummer's Eve party at your house. When it becomes dark, turn out all the main lights and switch on your torches and dance round, all holding hands. You must dance in a clockwise direction (the way the sun goes round) otherwise you'll have bad luck.

Midsummer Magic

Just before it gets dark, go out to the nearest waste land and look to see if you can find any ferns growing. They look like this:

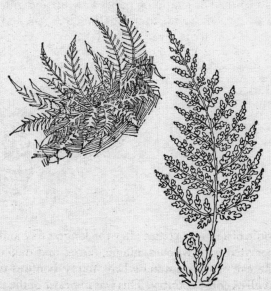

On the underside of the fern leaves there are hundreds of tiny fern seeds. Place a plate or saucer under the fern leaves and then shake the leaves. The tiny seeds will fall off and land in the plate.

It would be a good idea to have some cotton wool to put the seeds on, because they will stick to the cotton wool and not blow away in the wind.

Collecting the seeds is supposed to give the owner of the seeds the power of invisibility and protection against the fairies and witches that are supposed to dance on Midsummer's Eve. They are also supposed to give people good luck throughout the year and to give the owner the power of seeing into the future.

Keep some seeds for yourself and save some for later in your secret place. The best way to keep them is to put a few at a time on some cotton wool and put them in an empty matchbox.

Why don't you either paint the matchboxes or use some of your old Christmas wrapping paper to wrap and glue around the lid of the box to make it look better? You could get a sticky label and write on it.

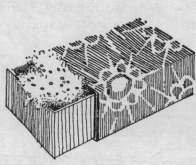

Stick the label on the lid of the box and store it away in your secret hiding place.

Ways of Telling the Future on Midsummer's Eve

To find if the one you love loves you, write down your name and your friend's name.

JANE MORGAN

JAMES STREETE

Cross out all the letters in both names that are the same. You can only use each letter once.

J̶A̶N̶E̶ M̶O̶R̶GAN

J̶A̶M̶E̶S̶ STR̶EETE

Count how many letters are left in each name.

1 2 345
J̶A̶N̶E̶ M̶O̶R̶GAN

1 23 4567
J̶A̶M̶E̶S̶ STR̶EETE

Now say Love, Friendship, Marriage, Hate, until you have reached the number that is the same as the number of letters left.

1 2 3 4 5
LOVE FRIENDSHIP MARRIAGE HATE LOVE

1 2 3 4 5 6 7
LOVE FRIENDSHIP MARRIAGE HATE LOVE FRIENDSHIP MARRIAGE

Then you have your answer:

Jane Morgan loves James Streete.
James Streete wants to marry Jane Morgan.

So now you know!

Roses are of special importance on Midsummer's Eve. It is said that any rose picked on Midsummer's Eve or Midsummer's Day will keep fresh until Christmas. Why don't you try to see if that is true?

At midnight on Midsummer's Eve, young girls should scatter rose petals before them and say:

> *Rose leaves, rose leaves,*
> *Rose leaves I strew.*
> *He that will love me*
> *Come after me now.*

Then the next day, Midsummer's Day, your true love will visit you.

Q. What did two male centipedes say to each other
   when they saw a lady centipede walk past?
A. What a lovely pair of legs, pair of legs, pair of legs,
   pair of legs . . .

Now, do you want to know what you will do in the future?

What to do: 1 Make a new pincushion by cutting out two
circles of black material about 5 in (12 cm)
in diameter.

2 Place the right sides of the circles together
and sew nearly all the way round using
small running stitches.

3 Turn the shape inside out and stuff it with
cotton wool or old tights cut up into small
pieces. You should make the pincushion
very thick.

4 Oversew the opening.

5 Mark your name on one side of the cushion
by inserting pins until only the heads show.

6 On the other side of the cushion use the
smallest pins you can find to make a circle
and then put a cross shape inside.

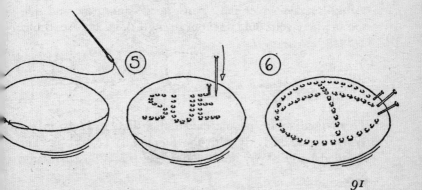

Now, when you go to bed at night, carefully put the pincushion in your right sock. Put the sock on the bottom of your bed and then you will dream of your future.

Midsummer's Day is a time when there are lots of fairs. Perhaps you could have a mock fair at lunchtime at school or at home after school. The old fairs years ago didn't have swings and roundabouts and things like that. They had things for sale – nice pots, pans, horses and geese and sideshows where you could test your strength or go and see strange sights.

Funny Sights

There used to be people called the 'Fattest Lady in the World' or 'The Lady with the Elephant's Trunk' or 'The Bearded Lady'. Why don't you dress up as a bearded lady, a fat lady or the thinnest man in the world? Then you could get a friend to shout, 'Roll up, roll up, see the Bearded Lady,' and let everyone peep at you – one at a time.

Old fairs were places where a lot of things were sold so, instead of actually selling things, why don't you bring out all the old things you don't want and try to swap them with some of your friends' old things?

Gingerbread Men

Gingerbread men were sold at fairs. Why don't you make some gingerbread men for your friends?

You need: Sieve
Mixing bowl
Saucepan
Gingerbread man cutter or blunt knife
Baking tray
Greaseproof paper
Palette knife or fish slice

7 oz (225 g) plain flour
2 teaspoonful ginger powder
1 teaspoonful mixed spice
½ teaspoonful bicarbonate of soda
3 oz (75 g) soft brown sugar
3 oz (75 g) butter
2 tablespoonsful golden syrup
currants

What to do:

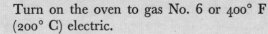

1. Turn on the oven to gas No. 6 or 400° F (200° C) electric.

2. Sieve the flour, spice, ginger and bicarbonate of soda into a bowl.

3. Melt sugar, butter and syrup in a saucepan until the mixture is runny but not too hot.

4. Pour this mixture into the bowl of flour, spices and bicarbonate of soda.

5. Mix into a paste.

6. Allow to cool a little, then the mixture will stiffen up into a dough.

7. Put the dough on a floured surface and roll out into a flat shape about ¼ in (5 mm) thick.

8. Either use a gingerbread man cutter or carefully cut the shape yourself with a blunt knife.

9. Then lift each shape carefully and put it on a baking tray covered with greaseproof paper. Don't put them too close together. This mixture should make quite a few gingerbread men. You may have to leave some out and bake them later.

10. Put currants on for eyes, nose, mouth and buttons.

11. Bake in the oven for 10 to 15 minutes. They should be a golden brown colour and slightly darker at the edges.

12. Remove from the oven with oven gloves and leave until cool. Remove from tray with a palette knife or a fish slice. Put on a plate and eat some and give some to your friends.

There are lots of games to play and things to do at your Midsummer Fair. See what else you can think up.

July

The July man rests under the leaves,
For the sun is high in the sky,
The air is sweet with summer smells,
And a busy bee flies by.

July is often the month that is hot and sleepy. It is nearly the end of term and summer holidays are near. But if it rains on July 1st, watch out, for there is an old saying which goes:

> If the first of July it be rainy weather,
> 'Twill rain more or less for four weeks together.

So let's hope that July 1st is always fine.

Work on the farm and in the house in the old days was very busy at this time of year and there wasn't much time for merriment, except for the occasional fair or saint's day celebrations. Children were required either to help or to amuse themselves.

Here are some games to play on the long summer evenings of July.

Follow My Leader

This is a game that can be played in town or country, though probably better in the town. It is a kind of treasure hunt.

The leader gets a head start by writing down in code where he will be going. For instance:

> Rt at S
> Left down T
> Left up R
> Rt. by the S. shop
> Next clue under big books in T.B.

This could mean:

> right at South Street,
> left down Topper Road,
> left up Redfern Road,
> right by the Sweet shop,
> next clue under the big books (telephone
> directories) in the Telephone Box.

It helps if you know the names of the streets around you and your right hand from your left.

The next clue could be something like 'Ask Mrs Policeman where I am.' That could mean that you all know the policeman's wife and would have to go and ask her for the next clue. (Make sure she doesn't mind helping!)

She could say something like, 'He's in the house with the red front door.' Then you'll have to stop and think! Who's got a red front door? It must be someone you all know otherwise the leader wouldn't be in the house. Do you know the colour of your own front door? Oh yes, it's red. Race home and the first one to find the leader wins the game and then has to be the leader himself.

Scavenger Hunt

This is a game I used to play a lot and now my children play it too.

Ask a grown-up to give you a list of five things to find.

Take the list and a bag to put your finds in and off you go.

First one to get all five is the winner and chooses the next five things to find.

Suggestions for things to choose:

1   Bus ticket
2   2p
3   Mars bar wrapper
4   Stone
5   Feather
6   Piece of fruit
7   Blue flower
8   Piece of wool
9   A bead
10   A leaf

Here are some more energetic games.

Jump Over

Tie a bean bag or an old soft toy to the end of a rope so that when the rope is swung round, the bag or toy acts as a weight.

Five or six people stand in a ring while the one with the bean bag and rope is in the middle of the circle. As the rope spins round everyone has to jump over it without touching the rope.

Of course, if the person with the rope is very clever he will change the speed of the rope every now and again to catch the others out.

With this game, don't be surprised if you get the odd whack on the ankle. It's only to be expected if you haven't jumped out of the way in time.

Piggy Stick

This game can only be played if you have a lot of space around you and there are no windows to break. So play it in a park or a field – or a play area.

You need: 1   A piggy stick – which is a stick of wood shaped like a pencil at the end. A cricket stump would do but it would be better if the wood was thicker. You can draw a snout and eyes and ears on it to make it look like a pig.

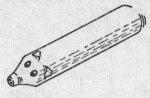

   2   A large flat stone or hard piece of flat earth.
   3   Another stick or a cricket bat.

The idea of the game is to put the piggy stick on the flat stone and then bang the snout of the piggy stick with the bat. This makes the piggy stick jump up into the air. The player then has to hit it as far as possible. When the stick has landed, the distance it has travelled is measured by counting how many steps there are between the starting stone and where the piggy stick lands. It is quite difficult to hit the piggy stick and anyone missing the stick more than three times is out.

If it does rain in July, here are some games you can make. Always make more than one, and put the spare ones carefully in your secret place.

Thaumatrope

This is a huge name for a small thing but it's simple to make and fascinating to play with.

You need:
    Cardboard
    Scissors
    Paints or felt tip pens
    String

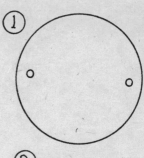

What to do:
1 Cut a 3 in (8 cm) circle out of the cardboard and make two holes near the edges opposite one another.
2 Draw or paint a small bird in the centre of one side.
3 Draw a bird-cage on the other side.
4 Cut two 10 in (25 cm) lengths of string. Thread them through the holes and tie the ends together so you have two loops.

Now the thaumatrope is finished.

To play:
Hold one loop in each hand. Spin the disc round so that the string gets wound up. Then pull the strings and watch the disc. It spins so fast that it looks as if the bird is in the cage.

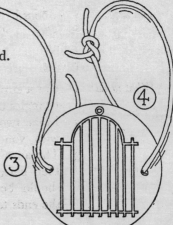

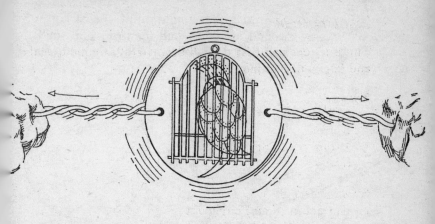

If you are very good at making thaumatropes, you could draw more designs, such as a goldfish one side and a bowl on the other; a box on one side and a jack-in-the-box on the other; a butterfly on one side and a net on the other.

Put one in your secret drawer till later.

Twizzer

This is made almost the same way as a thaumatrope.

You need: Cardboard
                Scissors
                Paint
                String

What to do: 1 Cut a circle out of the cardboard. Then cut triangles out of the edge of the circle.
             2 Make two holes in the middle and, if you wish, you can paint the card.
             3 Thread a piece of string through one hole then back through the other. (The string should be about 2 ft (60 cm) long.) Tie the ends together.

4 Spin the disc round until the string is
wound up. Then pull the string and you'll
find that the twizzer makes the sound of a
buzzing bee.

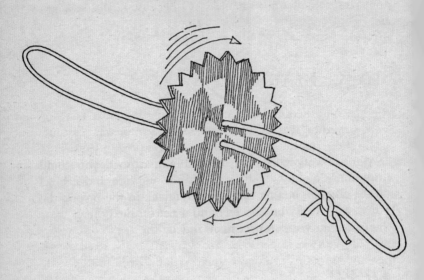

Make two twizzers and put one away for later.

July 15th is St Swithin's Day.

> *St Swithin's Day, if thou dost rain,*
> *For forty days it will remain.*
> *St Swithin's Day, if thou be fair,*
> *For forty days 'twill rain nae mair.*

Although it doesn't seem that rain on St Swithin's Day can
be a blessing, in some parts of Britain the rain is welcomed,
for it christens the apples on the trees and they should not
be picked until St Swithin's Day is over.

July 25th is St James' Day which is also known as Grotto Day. Children used to make grottoes and caves and decorate them with sea shells because the scallop shell is supposed to be the emblem of St James. The reason it became the emblem is not really known but some say it's because of this strange tale.

Story Time

St James had died and his body was being taken by boat to Spain where he was to be buried. A horseman was waiting on the shore for the boat to arrive. As the boat got close to the shore, the horse bolted into the sea, carrying its rider with him.

Miraculously, neither the rider nor the horse was drowned. It was said that the power of St James saved them but when the man and horse came out of the sea, both were covered with scallop shells. So, scallop shells have been the emblem of St James ever since. What do you think? Is it true?

Whether or not you think it's true, why don't you make a grotto on July 25th? If you have ever been to the seaside and have made a collection of shells, you could use some of them. If not, go to your local fishmonger and ask if he has any shells you may have.

There are all sorts of ways to make a grotto, but if you can't think of an idea, try this.

What to do: 1 Sprinkle a thin layer of earth in a tin tray or baking tray.
2 Make a cave using large stones, damp earth and moss.
3 Cover the cave grotto with shells.

4 Decorate the tray with shells and moss.
5 In the old days, a candle was placed in front of the grotto. You don't have to light it but it would look very nice if you could have a candle.

These grottoes were placed outside houses and the children would sit by them and say:

Please remember the Grotto.
It's only once a year.
Father's gone to sea.
Mother's gone to bring him back,
So please remember me.

If you cannot sit outside with your grotto, put it in the corner of a room and perhaps someone will light the candle for you when the evening comes.

Q. Why are fishmongers so mean?
A. Because their job makes them sell fish!

August

The August man with everyman
Rushes to cool by the sea;
His feet are bare, the sand is warm,
There's no happier man than he.

August 1st is Lammas Day, and the name Lammas comes from an Anglo-Saxon word *Hlafmaesse* which means Loaf Mass. The corn is being harvested at this time of year and so a loaf of bread could be made with the 'first fruits of the harvest'. This loaf was taken to church to be offered as a thanksgiving.

For some unknown reason, some farmers would let some of the first corn bread go stale and then crumble it over the corners of their barns. Perhaps it was to bring good luck to their barns as well.

Lammas Day was the beginning of another month of merry-making and happiness. In fact, it was the traditional month in which to get married or at least make marriage arrangements.

Lammas was also the time for farmers to give their farm workers a present of a pair of gloves. Perhaps the gloves were given so that the farm workers could have some protection for their hands during the hard days ahead, bringing in the harvest. In Exeter, a large white glove was put on the end of a long pole which was decorated with flowers and held on high to let the people know that the merriment of Lammas Fair was beginning.

Why don't you cut out the shape of a glove in white paper and hang it on your front door surrounded by flowers for Lammas Day?

It is easy to cut out a glove. All you have to do is put one of your hands on a piece of paper, draw round it and then cut out the shape. Cut out two hand shapes so that they look like a pair of gloves.

Stick them together at the top and pin on a flower. Then stick the whole thing to your front door. And if that isn't a popular idea, stick it to your bedroom door.

The first week in August is very important in Wales, for it is the week of the National Eisteddfod. An eisteddfod (pronounced *eye-sted-fod*) is a meeting of poets. There is a lot of music and dancing and competitions of all kinds during the week. One of the main competitions is to choose the best poem. Why don't you write a poem, or even start a poetry competition during this week? Hold your own local eisteddfod. Ask someone to judge your poems, and, as the Welsh do in their meetings, put a crown on the winner's head and let him sit on a special chair.

A recently published book called *I Like This Poem* contains poems that children like best and it has one of my favourites in it.

Cats*
by Eleanor Farjeon

Cats sleep
Anywhere,
Any table,
Any chair,
Top of piano,
Window-ledge,
In the middle,
On the edge,
Open drawer,
Empty shoe,
Anybody's
Lap will do,
Fitted in a
Cardboard box,
In the cupboard
With your frocks —
Anywhere!
They *don't care!*
Cats sleep
Anywhere.

* From *The Children's Bells*, published by Oxford University Press.

If you're going away on holiday in August, a lot of time is spent travelling, so you need to have something to occupy yourself. Here are a few games to play in the car.

Silly Willy

This game really made me cross when I first played it because I couldn't work it out but when I'd got it, I loved it!

Someone who knows the rules says something like, 'Silly Willy likes books but not magazines. What does Silly Willy like?'

Silence . . . looks of blank amazement from people who don't know the game. Then the person says again, 'Silly Willy likes bread but not cake. What does Silly Willy like?'

Silence . . . Thoughts of, 'I don't care what Silly Willy likes – he's stupid!'

Then again. 'Silly Willy likes bacon but he doesn't like ham. What does Silly Willy like?'

Crank, crank goes the brain – there's something stirring in the mind.   Silly Willy likes . . . books, not magazines,

bread, not cake,

bacon, not ham.

Aha! Cough, cough! Silly Willy only seems to like things beginning with B, is that it? Yes!

Oh, what a super game! Can I have a go? (I didn't know I could change my mind so quickly!) Have you got it yet? Have a go at these. The answers are at the end of the chapter.

Silly Willy likes boots but not shoes.
Silly Willy likes sheep but not lambs.
Silly Willy likes apples but not oranges.

or

Silly Willy likes the grass but not the street.
Silly Willy likes peas but not carrots.
Silly Willy likes leaves but not flowers.

or   Silly Willy likes soap but not water.
       Silly Willy likes boats but not ships.
       Silly Willy likes coal but not coke.

Here's another game that I first played when I was on
Playaway. I don't know what it is called, so I'll call it . . .

Where Are You Going?

It's a game using the letters of the alphabet in the order in
which they come. The first person has to say – I am going to
*A*ppleby to *a*sk *A*untie for *A*pples. The second player then has
to use the next letter which is B (clever . . . clever . . .). I am
going to *B*righton to *b*uy *b*ig *b*uns, and so on until someone is
caught out. It's got to make fairly good sense. If the game
goes very well, watch out for the awful letters like Q and
V and X. I'm going to *V*enice to *v*eil *V*enetian *v*indows will
not do!

I Went to the Shops

This is a similar game.

You start the sentence off with, 'I went to the shops and I
bought a ————' but you mime the thing you bought,
you don't say it. So, if the thing you bought was a toothbrush, you would mime cleaning your teeth.

The next player says, 'I went to the shops and bought
a ———— (mimes toothbrush) and a ————, (then
mimes another thing, like a car). This can be done by
pretending to steer a wheel and then pressing an imaginary
hooter. The next player says what he went to the shop to
buy and he too has to mime the toothbrush and car before
he can choose his own item.

Players have to drop out of the game every time they forget
something.

This is a good game to play in a traffic jam because people in the other cars will think you have gone mad!

Q. What is yellow and goes slam, slam, slam, slam?
A. A four door banana!!!

When your journey is over, the holiday's begun. Don't forget to collect anything that might be useful for your secret hiding place, such as shells for Grotto Day, unusual flowers to press, a small container of sand, and pebbles with unusual colours or shapes.

If you find a stone with a hole in it, thread it on to a piece of string and wear it round your neck. It is supposed to be very lucky and to protect you from witches. In fact, if you find a few stones with holes in, take them home and put them in your secret place.

When you are packing and sorting things out for your holiday – if your home is anything like my home – that's the time when you find *odd socks*. You know, those socks that have stayed loyal to you, whilst their other halves have wandered off. Here's a toy you can make.

Snake Puppet

You need: A sock
            A pencil
            Buttons or circles of material or both
            Needle and cotton
            Odd bits of material
            Stiff material or paper
            Scissors
            Glue

What to do: 1 First of all, put the sock on your hand with your thumb where the heel should be, fingers where the toes should be and the rest of the foot of the sock folded into your hand.

2 Then turn your fingers towards you. Bend them a bit and in the gap between the first and second finger make a mark with a pencil and another mark between the third and fourth fingers. The mark comes about where the second joint is on your finger.

3 Now take the sock off and sew a button to each of the marks. (Make sure you don't go through to the other side of the sock or you won't be able to get your hand in it.)

Or stick a circle of material or paper on the marks.

Or stick a large circle and a small circle on each mark.

Or stick a large circle on and sew a button in the middle.

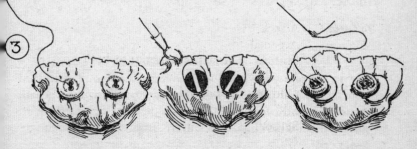

4 Now cut a long strip of stiff material or paper about 2×8 in (5×20 cm) and cut a shape out of one end like this.

5 Half way between the toe and the heel of the sock, stick or sew in the material. You could also stick on two small circles near the finger tips to make nostrils.

If you wriggle your hand and fingers about you'll find that your snake puppet soon has a character all his own. I call mine Silas and every time he says something beginning with an 's', he makes it hiss. 'Sssssurely, ssssausages are ssssimply ssssuper.'

You could make many more animals to go with Silas, just by adding different things, like ears or whiskers. Here is another idea for a sock puppet.

Elephant Puppet

You need:

A pair of old grey socks
Scissors
Needle and cotton

What to do:

1 Cut the toe off one sock and cut around the curve to make two ear shapes. Sew them into position.

2 Make a hole in the toe of the other sock and push your longest finger through.

3 Cut the foot off the spare sock and pull the leg part through the hole where your finger is. Use your finger to move the 'trunk'.

If you sit under a table, you can give a good puppet show by raising your arms as the puppets act.

If you have a younger brother or sister, put on a show for them and it will amuse them for ages. Don't forget to put some puppets away in your secret place for later.

Silly Willy answers

　　boots not shoes
　　sheep not lambs
　　a**pp**les not oranges
Silly Willy likes words with *double letters* in.

　　grass not street
　　peas not carrots
　　leaves not flowers
Silly Willy likes *green* things.

　　s**oa**p not water
　　b**oa**ts not ships
　　c**oa**l not coke
Silly Willy likes words with *oa* together.

September

Holiday's over, September man,
There's work to be done on the land,
Food to get ready for winter time,
There's no time to sit or stand.

This month has so many things to do and make. It is the most fruitful month of the year.

In September we celebrate the harvest. As the last of the wheat was gathered in, there used to be a lovely ceremony called 'Calling the Mare'. The farmers all wanted to prove they had the best reapers, so they tried to gather in the last of their crops before the neighbouring farmer did. The last sheaf of the harvest was used to make into a rough mare shape (a mare is a female horse) and it was quickly sent round to any farmer who had not finished gathering his crops. It was a way of saying to the farmer that wild horses would be after his crops if he didn't gather them in quickly. The men would run round to the neighbouring farm, throw the mare over the hedge into the field where the other farmer was working, and they would shout 'Mare, mare' and then run away.

Of course, once the men had received the mare, they had to work as quickly as they could to see if they could finish before another farm did, then they could throw the mare to them.

The farmer who was last to finish had to keep the mare all year and have it on display so that everyone knew he had been the slowest farmer that year.

Real straw can be hard to find but you could make a straw horse from drinking straws.

You need: 21 drinking straws
String or wool
Scissors
Felt-tip pen

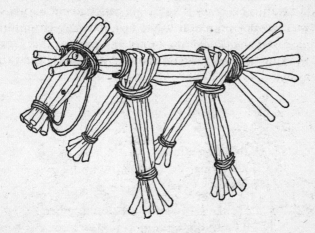

What to do: 1 Divide 18 of the straws into three bunches of six.

2 Take one bunch and tie it in two places about 2 in (5 cm) from each end. This makes the body.

3 Fold the other two bunches of straws round the body and tie them underneath.

4 Divide the bunches under the body into four legs and tie them above the 'ankles' to make the feet.

5 Take the three remaining straws and cut them in half. Put them together to make the head and tie them at one end to make the nose. Tie the head to the body as shown.

6 Draw eyes with a felt-tip pen and make a bridle out of wool.

Rather like the mare, there is a custom of making corn dollies. A corn dolly was supposed to have been the spirit of the corn goddess and dates back hundreds of years. In fact, it is a pre-Christian custom. People believed that the corn goddess lived in the corn and would die when the corn was harvested unless some of it was saved. So to make sure that the corn goddess stayed alive until the next spring sowing, a corn dolly was made from the last sheaf of corn for the corn goddess to rest in until the next.

Corn dollies are very hard to make but here is one that you might like to try.

You need: 9 drinking straws
Thin string or heavy cotton
Scissors

What to do: 1 Take six straws and carefully bend them in half. Bind some cotton round the straws about half an inch (1 cm) below the fold and tie it tightly. This is the head.

2 Now divide the straws into two bundles of six. Bind them near the bottom and tie them both tightly.

3 For the arms, cut the three remaining straws in half and poke them through the body. Bind and tie them at the 'wrists'. Keep the arms in place by binding the body crosswise as shown.

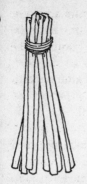 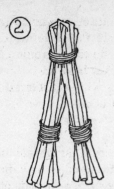 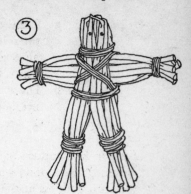

And there she is, a corn dolly. You can draw on a face if you like, and if you bend the legs a little, she should stand up easily. She says 'Hello' to the harvest time!

Make as many of these as you can, all the same size, and put them in your secret drawer. We'll find a use for them later.

P.S. You can make this doll the same way by using strands of wool.

After the harvest has been gathered in, it is time for the harvest supper. Here are some good things to cook.

Blackberry Flummery

You need: Saucepan
           Bowl
           Sieve
           Spoon

           1 lb (450 g) blackberries
           8 oz (225 g) sugar
           2 tablespoonsful cornflour
           Pinch of salt
           1 teaspoonful lemon juice

What to do: 1 Put the blackberries and sugar in a saucepan with just a little water and simmer
(that means warm through, but don't boil)
until the fruit is soft.

2 The next step is the bit I like doing best.
Get a bowl and a sieve. Sieve the blackberries and sugar, catching all the thick
juice in the bowl. Use the back of a spoon
and squeeze as much of the blackberries
through the sieve as you can.

3 Put the mixture in the saucepan.

4 Mix the cornflour and salt with two tablespoonsful of water.

5 Add this to the blackberries and simmer
again for five minutes.

6 Add the lemon juice and stir. Then pour
the mixture into a bowl and leave to cool.
This mixture sets as it cools. Eat it cold
with fresh cream!

Cinnamon Toast

At harvest time, there was always something made from
bread. This is a way of making toast that I learned when I
was in America. For some reason it makes a lovely popping,
crackling noise as it is cooking.

You need: 4 slices of bread
2 teaspoonsful cinnamon powder
2 teaspoonsful sugar
Butter

What to do: 1 Put the bread under the grill and toast both
sides a golden brown.

2 Mix the sugar and cinnamon together.

3 Butter the toast.

4 Sprinkle the cinnamon and sugar mixture over the toast.

5 Put back under the grill. Listen for the crackling sound and leave it for about one minute.

6 Take it out and eat it!

Sunshine Salad

Cucumbers, marrows and pumpkins are also traditional English harvest supper foods and so, of course, are apples. Marrows and pumpkins are quite difficult to cook, but here is an easy salad that you can make with cucumbers and apples.

You need: A bowl

2 hard-boiled eggs
2 mushrooms
2 oz (60 g) sultanas
2 apples
Half a cucumber
Pinch of salt and pepper
2 oz (60 g) salad cream
2 tomatoes

What to do: 1 Take the shells off the hard-boiled eggs.

2 Wash the mushrooms and sultanas.

3 Peel the apples.

4 Chop the cucumber, eggs, apples and mushrooms into slices and put them all into the same bowl.

5 Add the sultanas, a pinch of salt and a little pepper and the salad cream. Stir it all up with a spoon.

6 Slice the tomatoes and lay them on top in a pattern.

7 Eat with your supper or with . . .

Jacket Potatoes

You need: 1 medium potato per person
Butter
Cheese

What to do: These are very, very simple to make. All you have to do is scrub the potatoes and put them in the oven at 400° F (200° C) or gas No. 6 for about 40 minutes or until a skewer can be poked into them without the insides feeling hard. Remove from the oven with oven gloves. Put the potatoes on a plate. Cut each potato half way through, put a pat of butter in the middle and a slice of cheese too, if you like.

Harvest time joke

Once a farmer had a large hay field. His son was not happy in the country, so he moved to town to look for a job. The only job he could get was shining shoes, so now the farmer makes hay while the son shines.

Conkers

Conkers are the fruit of the horse-chestnut tree. Children have been playing with conkers for years. The idea is to get the biggest conker possible, make a hole in it, thread string through the conker, knot it at one end, then take it in turns with a friend to hold your conker up in the air while the friend tries to smash your conker with his conker.

I used to play this when I was at school, but I wasn't too good at aiming and many times, instead of hitting my friend's conker, I would miss and my conker would spin round and smash my knuckles.

Here's something else to do with conkers and acorns.

You need: Small conkers
                Acorns
                Thread or string or coloured ribbon

What to do: Make holes in the conkers and acorns. (You
                may need help with this.) Thread the ribbon
                through the holes. Tie a knot in the two ends
                and put it round your neck. It's a necklace of
                autumn.

You could make several and give them away to your friends – but don't forget to put one away in your secret hiding place. Wrap it up in newspaper to make sure it keeps dry.

On the first Monday after September 4th, in a town called Abbots Bromley in Staffordshire, a very picturesque custom takes place. It is called the Horn Dance. Six men hold masks on sticks which have long reindeer horns attached to them.

There are two teams of three men each. One team's reindeer horns are painted white – the other's are blue. Each team dances towards the other as if to fight, then they go back, then advance as if to lock horns, and then go back again. After a while they pass each other straight over to the other side and they start again.

There are other people in attendance dancing as well – a hobby horse, someone dressed as Maid Marion, a boy with a bow and arrow, a triangle player, a musician and a Fool.

Although you can't have the real horns to dance with, it might be fun for twelve of you to dress up and dance. You could use branches for horns and tie them on to a stick. For the hobby horse, you can use the one you made in May. Maid Marion wears a long dress. Make a bow out of a twig and some string for the boy with the bow and arrow. The Fool can be dressed to look like a clown with a red nose and someone else can play a triangle while the musician can bang a drum.

Home-made antlers

Then you are all ready to dance your own version of the Horn Dance to bring luck to all your friends.

No one really knows why the people of Abbots Bromley do their dance. Some say it celebrates a gift of woodland from

Henry I but other people say it is an old magical custom whose meaning has been forgotten.

> Q. What did the stag say to his children?
> A. 'Hurry up, deers.'

On September 18th at Crabapple Fair in Egremont, Cumbria, a fabulous gurning competition takes place. To gurn has many meanings but one of them is to 'distort the face' and making faces is just what the competition is – to see who can make the most awful face. You could have your gurning competition and see how many awful faces you can pull. Get someone to judge you.

Here are two things to make in September.

Pot Pourris

As September draws to a close, most of the flowers start to die in the colder weather. Collect as many petals as you can, dry them with a tissue and put them on a flat tray lined with tissue in a warm place (like an airing cupboard or near a radiator). Get some orange, lemon and tangerine peel, cut it up into fine strips and leave them to dry.

When the petals and the peel are dry and a little 'crispy', put them all together in a pretty bowl. Sprinkle them with a teaspoonful of ground cloves and a teaspoonful of ground allspice and mix them together. This keeps your room smelling sweet. Every time you pass the bowl, turn the petals over and release their perfume into the air. If you have made more than you need, put some in small polythene bags, label them POTPOURRI – AUTUMN FLOWERS, and put them away in your secret drawer.

Suggested flowers to use for petals
Roses
Lavender
Blue Hydrangeas
Honeysuckle
Orange blossom
Any herbs that you can find

Lavender Bags

You need: Two squares of material about 4 × 4 in
(10 × 10 cm)
Needle and cotton
Lavender flowers

What to do: 1 Put the right sides of the material together
and sew round three sides of the square.
  2 Turn the bag inside out and fill it with the
lavender flowers.

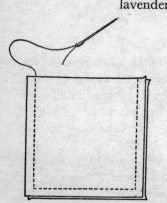
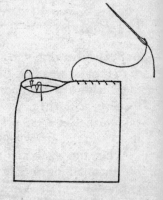

  3 Complete the bag by turning the open
edges inside and over-sewing them.

Lavender bags make clothes smell nice if you put them in
wardrobes or drawers. Make quite a few and put them in
your secret hiding place for later.

October

Gather the apples, October man,
And the autumn leaves need clearing,
The days are short, the nights are long,
And Hallowe'en is nearing.

This is one of my favourite months. The leaves are falling off the trees and form a multicoloured carpet on the ground, while mists and early fogs swirl around setting the scene for *ghosts* and *ghoulies*.

In Hampshire, in the eighteenth century, a Mr William Davis was riding home when a heavy fog surrounded him, and in no time at all he found that he had lost his way. Suddenly, he heard the bells from his church start to ring, so he followed the sound and got safely home.   Later on he worked out that he must have been only a few yards away from the chalk pits, where the ground had been dug deeply. Had he gone on any further, he would have been killed. When Mr Davis died in 1754, he left some money in his will. The money was to pay bellringers to ring the church bells at 6.30 a.m. and 7 p.m. on October 7th every year, to help travellers find their direction should they be lost on the same night as he had been lost.

Why don't you make some bells on this day to remember Mr Davis?

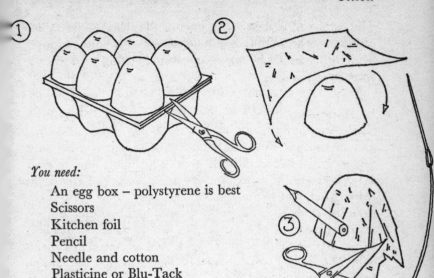

You need:

> An egg box – polystyrene is best
> Scissors
> Kitchen foil
> Pencil
> Needle and cotton
> Plasticine or Blu-Tack
> Beads
> Twigs
> Old newspaper
> Silver paint

What to do:

1 Carefully cut one of the half egg shapes from the egg box. Trim round the bottom for your bell shape.

2 Cut a 5 in (12 cm) square of kitchen foil and cover the bell shape.

3 Gently smooth the sides with the base of a pencil and trim the bottom. Then remove the tin foil bell.

4 Thread 12 in (30 cm) of cotton on to the needle. Double it and tie a knot at the end. Stick a small ball of plasticine over the knot and thread a bead on to the cotton. The plasticine should be big enough to stop the bead falling off.

Put another ball of plasticine about 1 in (2 cm) above the bead.

5 Push the needle through the centre of the tin foil bell and pull the cotton through until you reach the first ball of plasticine. Cut the cotton about 4 in (10 cm) above the top of the bell and tie a knot.
Make several more bells.

6 Get some twigs and, making sure that you put old newspaper down first, paint them silver.

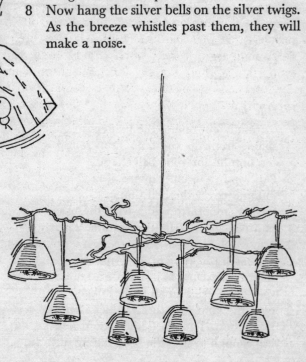

7 When the paint is dry, cross one twig over the other and tie them together with white cotton. Make a loop from the cotton to hang the mobile up.

8 Now hang the silver bells on the silver twigs. As the breeze whistles past them, they will make a noise.

As well as hanging this in your room in October, you could use it as a Christmas decoration.

> Knock, knock.
> Who's there?
> Bell.
> Bell who?
> Belt up and I'll tell you!

The beginning of October used to be the time for 'Mop' or Hiring Fairs. Servants and farm labourers would work from October to October and then all go to the centre of the village or town to hire themselves out again for the next year. They would be dressed in their best clothes, and to let people know what work they wanted, they used to wear or carry some sign of their work. Maids would carry a small mop (that's where we get the name Mop Fairs from), a cowman had a plait of cow hair in his lapel or in his hat, a shepherd had wool, a gardener had flowers and so on. The new masters and mistresses would walk around the fair and talk to the people. When they had come to an agreement, they gave the servant a small token – maybe something like 5p. The servant would then remove the sign of his job and replace it with a bunch of brightly coloured ribbons to let everyone else know that he had been hired.

The modern thing is 'Bob a Job'. Why don't you do odd jobs on the first Saturday in October? Pin on your coat the sign of the job you want to do:

A leaf for clearing leaves from paths.
A duster for dusting.
A dog's lead – to take the dog for a walk.
A dish cloth for washing up, and so on.

Perhaps you could make up a rhyme too, something like:

>*Today is the day of the Hiring Fair.*
>*I'll do my work with lots of care.*
>*Look at my sign to see what I'll do:*
>*I'll change it to ribbons when I am through.*

Then when the job is over, if you've managed to earn 5p, put your ribbons on your coat, join your friends and buy yourself a present. You've earned it!

> Knock, knock.
> Who's there?
> Bob.
> Bob who?
> Bob a job, can I help you?

Punky Night

Punky Night is the last Thursday in October and is a Somerset tradition. Some time in the Middle Ages, all the men of Hinton St George went off to a fair. When they failed to return that evening, the women went looking for them by the light of *punkies*. Punky is another name for a pumpkin which has been hollowed out and has a candle standing inside it. Nowadays, on Punky Night, there is a competition to see who has made the best punky and the children say or sing these verses:

>*It's Punky Night, tonight.*
>*It's Punky Night, tonight.*
>*Give us a candle, give us a light.*
>*It's Punky Night, tonight.*

>*It's Punky Night, tonight.*
>*It's Punky Night, tonight.*
>*Adam and Eve wouldn't believe*
>*It's Punky Night, tonight.*

Why don't you make a punky?

You need: A pumpkin (but a swede or turnip will do)
A candle
String

What to do: 1   Get someone to cut the top off the pumpkin. (This can be quite hard, so you may need help.)

2   Scoop out the inside of the lid and the inside of the pumpkin. Don't throw it away – someone might like to make a pie from it.

3   Wipe the pumpkin dry with some tissue.

4   Using a knife, carefully cut out different shapes around the pumpkin to make a face.

5   Make two holes near the top of the pumpkin. Thread string through to make a handle, then tie the ends of the string together.

6   Get a 'nite-lite' candle – the short, fat type, and put it in the pumpkin.

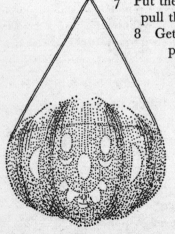

7   Put the lid back on the pumpkin and pull the handle up.

8   Get someone to light the candle by putting a lighted taper through one of the holes you've made. Switch out the lights and look at the punky.

Perhaps you could have a competition to see who has made the best one.

And now we've come quite near to *Hallowe'en* – October 31st – and we should start making things to celebrate it. It is supposed to be a time when witches and ghosts are about. Save the pumpkin from Punky Night, as we can use him again on Hallowe'en.

Witch's Broomstick

What to do: 1   Gather up any old fallen twigs.
                2   Put them in a bundle and tie them together with string.
                3   Push a larger twig or stick into the middle of the twigs.

Witch's Hat

You need: Black paper about 17 in (42 cm) square
            Tape measure
            Scissors
            Kitchen foil
            Glue and sellotape
            Black wool, material or paper

What to do: 1 On the square of black paper, use the tape measure to make a line of dots 17 in from one of the top corners. Join up the dots and cut along the line.

2 It is easiest to decorate the hat while it is still flat. Cut a star and a moon shape out of kitchen foil and glue them to the front of the hat.

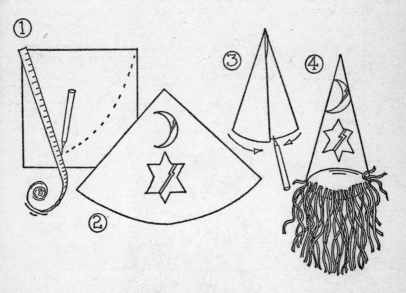

3 Bend the straight sides round to make a cone and try it on for size. Get someone to mark where the join comes. Take the hat off and glue it to fit you. (You might need to use some sellotape inside to hold it firmly.)

4 All you have to do now is stick strands of wool or narrow strips of black material or paper inside the edge of the hat to hang down the back.

Witch's Cloak

You need: A large piece of black crepe paper or material about 2 yds (2 m) square
                Scissors

What to do: Fold the paper or material in half and cut a semi-circle from the middle of the fold. When you open the material out, you will find a circle big enough to put your head through.

Now you're a completely dressed witch and you're ready to play some Hallowe'en games!

Daddy, there's a black cat in the dining-room.
Don't worry, son – black cats are lucky.
You're so right. This one's eaten your fish and chips.

Hallowe'en Games

Bobbing for Apples

1 Place three or four apples in a large bowl of water.
2 Put newspaper on the floor and then put the bowl of apples on top.
3 Kneel on the floor around the bowl with your hands behind your back.
4 Take it in turns to lean forward and try to get an apple out of the water using only your mouth.
   Have a towel handy for this game!

Here is another very similar game that doesn't involve water.

1 Tie a length of string from one chair to another.
2 Hang apples on strings from the main string.

3 Then as before, kneel with your hands behind your back and try to bite a piece out of the apple. WATCH OUT though! The apples are quite likely to swing and smack you in the face. Which makes you shout out 'CORE!' Oh dear, sorry!

If you want to keep witches away from you on Hallowe'en, here's what you do.

1 Pin garlic or a twig of rowan to your front door.
2 Wear blue, because it is the colour of the heavens. Witches don't like blue.
3 Put a new penny in your pocket.
4 Put a penny in each shoe.
5 Sew red thread into your clothes.
6 Wear your necklace with the hole stone.
7 Witches are only supposed to appear from midnight until dawn, when they will have to leave – so keep them busy. Put a used horseshoe outside the door. The witch cannot come in your house until she has travelled every inch that the horseshoe has travelled.

8 Put a large bowl outside the front door and pour salt in it. The witch may not come in until she has counted every grain.

Hallowe'en is another night when you are supposed to be able to tell the future. One way involves making a bowl of mashed potato and hiding a coin, a wishbone and a ring in amongst the mash. Give everyone present a dollop of mashed potato and see who gets the hidden goodies. Tell everyone that something is hidden in the mashed potato, otherwise *those who don't chew their food properly will swallow something they shouldn't*. Getting the ring means a happy marriage. Getting the wishbone means good luck, and getting the coin means you'll have money.

Discover the initial of the one who loves you.

Peel an apple so that the peel comes off in one strip. Throw the peel over your shoulder. When you turn round, the peel will have made the shape of a letter.
That letter will be the initial of your
loved one's name.

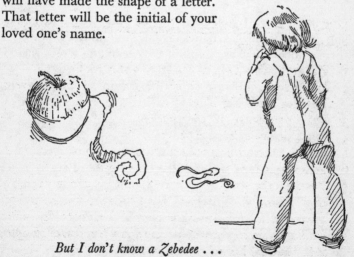

But I don't know a Zebedee . . .

Another way of finding your true love's name is to catch two snails. Put them under a box in the garden so they can't escape, and leave them overnight. When you lift the box in the morning, they will have written the name of your loved one.

Can you read snail writing?

One more thing. If you eat an egg on Hallowe'en, make sure you crush the shell. Witches love to hide in them – they use them as boats to chase ships on the ocean and wreck them if they can!

November

Fog wraps round November man,
It's cold and damp and dark;
A shi'ps horn blows far out at sea
And a lonely dog does bark.

November 1st is All Saints' Day and is traditionally the night when people disguise themselves. Why don't you have a fancy dress party and give a prize for the best costume? All the costumes have to be made by you and your friends – no cheating with help from adults.

November 2nd is All Souls' Day. This time of year is the time set aside for us to think about the people who have lived in the world before we have. In some parts of the country, All Souls' Day ends with a play or some songs and it is the time when children ask for a special cake called a 'Soul Cake'.

> *A soul, a soul, a soul cake,*
> *Please good missus, a soul cake.*
> *An apple, a pear, a plum or a cherry,*
> *Any good thing to make us merry.*
> *One for Peter, two for Paul,*
> *Three for Him who made us all.*

The 'Soulers' go around the houses singing this song and they are often joined by their old friend, the hobby horse – only at this time of the year, he is called the Hooden Horse.

A Soul Cake was like a hot cross bun but without the currants or the cross on top. So make the same recipe as we made in April for the hot cross buns. Leave out the currants, roll into balls of dough and flatten out before cooking.

November 4th has got a smashing name in some parts of the country – it's called Mischief Night. This was a night when all sorts of *naughty* things were done – the main idea being to put things in the wrong place.

The next bit is not for parents to read.

When everyone is asleep, why don't you . . .

1 Move some of the chairs to different places.
2 Hide all the slippers.
3 Hide the bread.
4 Put the knives and forks in a different drawer.
5 Hide the soap.

But – you've got to be very quiet *and you mustn't tell anyone that I gave you the idea!*

Fireworks

You must all know the dangers of fireworks by now, so don't get too near the bonfire or too near the fireworks and *never* hold a firework in your hand.

In my house, we all make a Guy Fawkes as big as we can and put it on the bonfire. Then the children and I stand by the back door and watch my husband light the bonfire and the fireworks, while we shout loud choruses of ooohs and aaaahs at the right time!

November

Food for Firework Night

Jacket potatoes are our favourite on Bonfire Night – and you know how to make them – they're in the September chapter.

Parkin is the traditional cake to eat on November 5th. Here is a very old recipe from Sheffield.

Mother's Parkin

You need: Mixing bowl
Baking tray

1 lb (450 g) oatmeal
4 oz (125 g) butter or lard
2 dessertspoonsful baking powder
2 teaspoonsful ground ginger
1 teaspoonful mixed spice
Golden syrup

What to do: 1 Heat the oven to 375° F (190° C) or gas No. 5.
2 Rub the butter into the oatmeal with your fingers.
3 Mix in the baking powder, spices and ginger.
4 Using a tablespoon of golden syrup at a time, mix in until you have made a thick paste.
5 Pour into a greased baking tray and cook for one hour.
6 Look at it every 20 minutes to make sure it doesn't burn.
7 Take out of the oven and leave to cool.
8 When cool, cut it into strips, put it on a plate and *eat* it!

A drink that goes very well with parkin is hot chocolate.

Here's my own recipe that I made up when I was eight years old. It's a sweet sticky drink but I loved it.

Hot Chocolate

1 Pour a cup of milk into a saucepan and heat until almost boiling.
2 Pour it into a mug.
3 Drop in half a bar of milk chocolate broken into bits (or a whole bar if you haven't eaten most of it while the milk was boiling).
4 Stir the milk until the chocolate has melted.
5 Drink it when it has cooled a little.

After I had made this successfully, I tried to make more drinks like it by adding sweets to hot milk. I can tell you – a packet of wine gums in milk is *awful*.

November is the time to start your Christmas cards. So go to your secret hiding place and sort out all those pictures from last year's cards that you kept.

Ideas for Christmas Cards

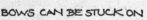

BOWS CAN BE STUCK ON

KNOT THE COTTON BEHIND THE CARD HERE

1 Get pieces of card or paper. Fold them in half and then stick your old pictures on the front.
2 Cut out stars and bell shapes in gold or silver paper and stick them on the front of your cards. You can decorate a bell shape by sticking a bow of ribbon on top. The clapper can be made by threading a bead on to some cotton and threading it through the card so that it hangs down.

3   Holly leaves can be cut out of green paper and berries can be added by sticking or sewing red beads to the card.

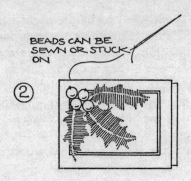

4   The Father Christmas and Christmas pudding are easy to draw as they are mostly circles. Father Christmas could have a red nose to match his hat – and why not stick a few real currants on the Christmas pudding?

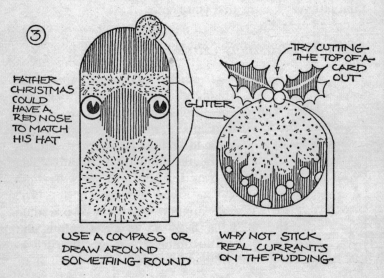

Don't forget to write really nice messages inside.

November 25th is supposed to be the night when children write letters to Father Christmas to wish him a Merry Christmas and to let him know the presents they would like. (That is if they've been good enough to deserve any.)

And even if you are not sure if Father Christmas exists, it's a good idea to write to him anyway – just in case!

Give the letter to one of your parents to post. If you have brothers or sisters who are too young to write, help them by asking what they want and writing it down for them.

Story Time

It was a dark winter's night and Sir Oswald came home to his castle. He had come home a day earlier than anyone expected and so all the servants were away – doing their Christmas shopping. Sir Oswald opened the door and it gave a loud c-r-e-e-e-a-k. He felt for the candle and the matches. He lit the first match but the wind blew the flame out. He lit another match, but the wind blew this out too. Finally, he managed to light the candle with the third match, which was just as well, for there were only three matches in the box. The candlelight cast eerie shadows over the main hall of the castle, making Sir Oswald feel uneasy.

He decided to go straight to bed. As he started to climb the creaking stairs, he heard a noise from far off in the castle. RAP! RAP! ... RAP! RAP!

It seemed to be coming from the other end of the corridor. He walked slowly past the bedrooms to the servants' part of the castle – at the end of the corridor. Now, Sir Oswald had never been in this part of the castle before. He heard the noise again. RAP! RAP! ... RAP! RAP!

It seemed to be coming from a small door on the left. He opened the door and found that it led to a staircase that spiralled up and up.

'It must lead to the top of a turret,' thought Sir Oswald and, as he started to climb the stairs, he heard the noise again, only louder. RAP! RAP! . . . RAP! RAP!

Up and up the stairs he went, until he came to a door at the top. He opened it. The noise was much louder! RAP! RAP! . . . RAP! RAP!

He lifted the candle and shone the light around the room. It was empty except for a tall thin cupboard. RAP! RAP! . . . RAP! RAP!

The noise seemed to come from inside the cupboard. Sir Oswald walked towards it, opened the door . . . and there it was . . . a piece of wrapping paper!!! Then his candle went out.

December

Time to go home, December man,
Home to your family and friends,
To sing and be merry at party time
As the old year ends.

Now is the time to make good use of all those things you made two of during the year. Did you guess what they were for? Yes, they were for Christmas presents, so let's see what you've got to give away.

1 A pomander
2 A ball and cup game
3 Peg dolls
4 Scented soap bag
5 Varnished eggs
6 Egg gift boxes (put a sweet in these)
7 Cotton reel dragon
8 Bottle of May Dew
9 Pressed flower pictures
10 Lucky fern seeds
11 Thaumatrope
12 Twizzer
13 Lucky hole stone necklace
14 Sock puppets
15 Corn dollies
16 Conker and acorn necklace
17 Pot pourri
18 Lavender bag

Christmas Decorations

A lot of people make their own Christmas decorations out of tinsel and coloured paper and anything bright and shiny. However, Christmas decorations a long time ago were made mainly from branches of trees or bushes. People used to think that when everything else was dying in winter time, the evergreens were symbols of undying life.

A vase of evergreen branches with some red holly berries peeping through looks really good at Christmas. You could brighten it up even more by painting a few twigs from other trees gold or silver.

It was supposed to be very lucky to have both holly and ivy in the house. Holly with its red berries brought good luck to the men in the house and ivy was supposed to bring good luck to the women.

Mistletoe is my favourite decoration at Christmas. I suppose you know that if you catch someone standing under the mistletoe, you can give them a kiss. Well, years ago, every time a kiss was taken under the mistletoe, a berry from the branch had to be removed, so you could only have as many kisses as there were berries on the mistletoe. So get loads of it!

Why don't you make a mistletoe bough?

Mistletoe boughs or kissing boughs, as they were sometimes called, were hung from the ceilings of many rooms. They are very pretty and easy to make.

You need: Two old wire coat hangers
Blu-Tack
String
Sellotape
Holly and/or ivy
Tinsel
Green crepe paper
Kitchen foil
Scissors
Mistletoe

What to do:

1 Bend the wire from the hangers into two hoops and put one inside the other so that they look like this. (Get someone to help you with this because the hook has to be removed and it could be a bit dangerous.)

2 Fix the hoops together at top and bottom with Blu-Tack and then tie them with string.

3   Then tie or stick (with sellotape) the holly and/or ivy all around the hoops.

4   Twist some tinsel (and green crepe paper) around the hoops as well.

5   Cut out some bells from silver foil or make some the same way as you did in October. Thread string through the top and hang this in the centre of the two hoops.

6   Get a bunch of mistletoe, with as many berries as possible, and tie it into a bunch.

7   Hang the bunch of mistletoe from the bottom of the hoops. Then get someone to hang it up for you. When anyone stands underneath it . . . give them a kiss!

Every Christmas, the postman is rushed off his feet delivering Christmas cards. Sometimes there just don't seem to be enough places to put them all. We don't stand them up on window ledges or mantelshelves because they keep falling down. We make them into long colourful streamers.

You need: Green ribbon or crepe paper
Christmas cards
Paper clips
Drawing pins

What to do:

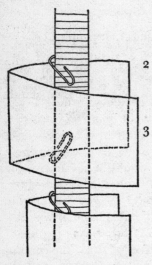

1 Cut lengths of ribbon or crepe paper long enough to hang from just below the ceiling to about half way down the wall – about 1½ yds (1.25 m).

2 Put the ribbon on a table and attach the back of each card at the top and bottom with paper clips.

3 Then put a drawing pin through the top of the ribbon and pin it to the wall.

By the way, did you know that Christmas cards were first sent only in Victorian times? Before that people would sometimes write a verse message to someone to wish them a Happy Christmas, but there were no cards.

The first well-known Christmas card was made by J. C. Horsley for Sir Henry Cole in 1846 and Sir Henry had a thousand copies made to send to his friends. The idea caught on and people have been sending Christmas cards to each other every year since. In fact, in 1975, an American sent 62,824 cards to his friends. He must know a lot of people but fancy licking all those stamps. Ugh!

Think of a number between 1 and 50. Double it.
Take away 61. Add 1. Subtract the number you
first thought of. Close your eyes.
DARK, ISN'T IT?!!

Yule Log

In years gone by, one of the first things that people began to
prepare for Christmas was the Yule Log. (Yule is another
word for Christmas.) It must have been a bit frightening
years and years ago when the weather got colder and nearly
all the plants died. People used to cut down a huge log of
ash, oak or fruit tree and bring it into the house on Christmas
Eve. Then it was ceremoniously lit and it had to stay alight
for at least twelve hours. If it went out at all during these
hours it meant that the next year would be a bad one for
farmers, because there would be little sun and so little
harvest that the people would go hungry. So you can imagine
how hard they worked to keep the flames alight. It was also
supposed to be unlucky for anyone to buy a yule log, for it
meant that they wouldn't work hard enough for the coming
harvest. So everyone had to cut and prepare their own yule
log.

Why don't you make a yule log?

You need:　A small but thick branch or piece of wood. Holly and ivy and any other Christmas decorations you can find. Why not use some of the gold oak leaves you painted in May?

What to do:　All you have to do is stick holly or ivy in or around the log and put anything else that looks good on it as well. If the branch has a 'knot' or hole in it, put a candle there. Then the candle can be lit when you are having your Christmas dinner.

Mumming Plays

Some of the oldest things that still happen in parts of the country at Christmas are Mumming Plays. These were plays in which people dressed up, completely masking themselves, and acted out a struggle or fight between darkness and light. This was because people were frightened of the darkness of winter and they wanted to get rid of winter as soon as possible so that the sun would come back.

The 'baddie' (or winter) is usually someone dressed all in black and the 'goodie' (summer) is someone dressed in white, or white and red. Some of the characters have become a bit muddled up over the years, but basically every play has a villain and a hero. The villain kills the hero but a doctor appears and magically cures the hero. The villain creeps away and then there is a dance and everyone is happy.

Why don't you do your own mumming play?

Traditionally, the costumes are made of long strips of paper or rag sewn or stuck all over some old clothes. The hat usually has long streamers too.

December

What to do:

1   Make a hat like the witch's hat you made in November and cover it with strips of light-coloured paper or material. Make the strips long enough to cover your face so that you are in disguise.

2   Make a circle of ribbon to tie loosely round your neck and hang long ribbons of the same colour from that.

3   The hero and villain need sticks of wood as swords to fight with.

4   The doctor needs a bag full of pretend medicines – like a bottle of water, toy frog, talcum powder, a mallet to knock the patient's knees with and anything else you can think of!

The characters

VILLAIN – dressed in black

HERO – dressed in white

DOCTOR – dressed in green

FATHER CHRISTMAS – dressed in red and white (Nobody is quite sure how he got into the play.)

LITTLE JACK – dressed in any colour (He is to be the story teller.)

You can write your own script and give your villain and hero their own names. Here's a rough guide for you. You can make it as long or as short as you like.

LITTLE JACK:
>   In come I, Little Johnny Jack,
>   I see the winter has come back,
>   But rain or snow won't keep me away,
>   I've come to see your Mummers Play.
>   Ladies and gentlemen, give what you please,
>   Give it to old Father Chrissymas, please.

FATHER CHRISTMAS:
> In come I, old Father Christmas,
> Welcome or welcome not,
> I hope old Father Christmas
> Will never be forgot!
> Although we've got but a short time to stay,
> We've come to show you a jolly old play.
> In comes our hero dressed in white,
> He's bold Sir George, yes, George the Knight.

SIR GEORGE:
> In come I, St George the bold,
> Oh, I say, this country's cold.
> I've been away to warmer lands,
> Fighting a dragon with my hands.
> I at last brought him to slaughter
> And now I'll marry the King's fair daughter.

BLACK KNIGHT:
> In come I, the Black, Black Knight,
> I've nothing to do so I fancied a fight.
> I'll fight St George, he's supposed to be strong,
> But between you and me, he won't live long!

[*St George and the Black Knight take out wooden swords and fight. The Black Knight wins. St George falls to the ground. The audience shouts out 'Aaaah!'*]

DOCTOR:
> In come I, the good Doctor Chubb,
> I'll wake Sir George with my strong club.
> [*Pretends to bash George with the mallet, but actually hits the floor to make a loud sound.*]
> I'll sprinkle him with lots of water
> To make him fit for the King's dear daughter.
> I'll put some powder on his head,
> Rise up, Sir George, you're no longer dead.

[*Cheers from audience.*]

FATHER CHRISTMAS
and LITTLE JACK:

> Hurray! Hurray! Our play is done,
> Black Knight has lost, Sir George has won,
> We can no longer wait around here,
> Merry Christmas and a Happy New Year.

You could go round to your neighbours' houses and do this play for them. It makes a nice change from carol singing.

At last Christmas Day comes and you have all the pleasure of unwrapping your presents and seeing other people unwrap theirs.

Have a lovely Christmas — and don't forget to save those Christmas cards, wrappers and strings for next year. You know why now, don't you?

BYE!

Index